GOD

BLESS

MINNEAPOLIS

GOD

BLESS

MINNEAPOLIS

LOOKING ABOVE AT BLESSINGS

JEAN MAHLUM

cbe
publishing LLC
Glyndon, MN

© 2010 Jean Mahlum

Published by
cbe publishing LLC
Glyndon, MN

Publisher's Cataloging-in-Publication Data
Mahlum, Jean.

   God bless Minneapolis : looking above at blessings / Jean Mahlum. — Glyndon, MN : cbe Pub. LLC, 2010.

   p. ; cm.

   ISBN13: 978-0-692-01134-8

   1. Mahlum, Jean. 2. Women with disabilities— Minnesota—Minneapolis. 3. Faith. I. Title.

   HV3013.M34 A3 2010
   362.43092–dc22   2010935866

FIRST EDITION

Cover design by Chris Rhoads
Interior design by Brooke Camfield

Printed in the United States of America
14   13   12   11   10   •   5   4   3   2   1

Dedication

First and foremost, a profound heartfelt "thank you" to the community of Minneapolis, and most particularly to all the wonderful people at the Hennepin County Medical Center, especially the dedicated personnel at the Hyperbaric Chamber.

A special thanks—one I can never repay—goes to Kathy Kennedy, the nurse who first informed me there was such a thing as hyperbaric medicine.

I also want to thank the Days Inn University employees in Minneapolis who became my family for five months, my dear Uncle Frank and Aunt Peg Gebhardt and family, Dr. Rodney Lee, Dr. Alex Lebrija, Dr. Brent Hella, Hannah, Lisa, and the Dakota Boys and Girls Ranch staff in Moorhead, Minnesota, Dr. David McNamara, the staff at the Super 8 Motel in Rochester, the Whitaker Wellness Institute, Dr. Kitaoka, Janelle DeGrote, Erin Mason, ProRehab, Dr. Rohla, Lowell Larson and the Fargo-Moorhead Master Chorale, Ken Kohler, the staff and students at Hawley High School, Ulen-Hitterdal High School, and Lake Park Audubon High School, and the staff and students at the Minnesota School of Business—Moorhead Campus.

Thank you also to all the dear people who prayed for me during a difficult time—my pastor and his wife, Rick and Carol Larson, and the members of the Dilworth, Minnesota, Presbyterian Church, and so many others who raised me up in their prayers. I owe you such gratitude. Please know my prayers encompass you as well, and I hope your lives continue to be a blessing to others.

So many people offered their assistance in my hour of need that I cannot begin to name them all. To the two people who most generously directed me toward the light, the stranger who boarded the Amtrak in downtown Minneapolis on November 5, 2007, and my dear, dear friend Pamela Kronbeck, thank you.

My family most of all deserves my thanks, and I thank God for you every day.

Wayne, my dear husband, you stood by me when the going wasn't easy, and I love you for it. Thanks be to God for all of you.

"It is good for me that I have been afflicted; that I might learn thy statutes. The law of thy mouth is better unto me than thousands of gold and silver. Thy hands have made me and fashioned me: give me understanding, that I may learn thy commandments. They that fear thee will be glad when they see me; because I have hoped in thy word. I know, O Lord, that thy judgments are right, and that thou in faithfulness hast afflicted me."

Psalm 71-75.

Contents

Prologue
Looking at a Changed Life

It is no small thing that I am here today. God bless Minneapolis. Thanks to you, my eyes have been opened. I mean, really opened. God bless Minneapolis.

For five months, you saw me stumbling around in the snow, ice on my crutches, my right foot dragging a cast, and you said, "I'll pray for you" or "God bless you" without knowing anything about me.

The lessons I learned in Minneapolis were huge, humbling, and life-changing, and I believe the story must be told. Not my story, but the story of God working in my life, and to Him be the glory.

In November of 2007, when I came to Minneapolis to receive services from Hennepin County Medical Center, I was a believer, but I was not nearly aware enough of how blessed I was.

I thought this would be a time of healing for the infected bones in my foot, but I discovered that healing took place in my soul as well. I believe all of this happened so that I could help others, and I pray that sharing the experiences that restored me physically and opened my heart and mind in ways I never could have imagined will benefit all who read about them.

I now wake up every morning thanking God for restoring my health and my faith. I want my story to inspire anyone who wonders whether God is watching, whether they are taken care of, and whether or not angels really do exist.

I have no doubt that they do. They are all around us, and often they are the most unlikely people. For who can they be but our fellow humans, sinners just like us, all children of God, no better and no worse?

Today, I know that angels are busy going about the Father's business in Minneapolis. They are you, all of you dear people. I now know that you were watching, guiding, leading me, praying for me, working for me, and offering me healing, hope, and love at a time when I was probably at my most unlovable. I regret that I can't thank you by name, but I pray you know who you are, and that your lives are as blessed as mine.

At the Hennepin County Hyperbaric Chamber in Minneapolis, I received life-giving oxygen, but I was also given a second chance at life and a new outlook on life. God bless you, downtown Minneapolis. It's a place I never wanted to go, believing that people there would not be concerned with others, much less someone like me, wandering about on crutches with an attitude that was…well, less than grateful for life.

I was trying to survive and hold on to a foot that had been marked for amputation. If only I had realized how blessed I was, perhaps I could have thanked you in some wordless way. But you have my heart, and my everlasting gratitude for not looking the other way, but for making a home for me. I was a stranger, and you took me in.

I wrote this book because I hope my story of redemption and humility may open someone else's eyes and heal them as well. I have been surrounded by a mighty cloud of angels, in a most unlikely place, for a most unlikely reason. As time goes on, I am limping less. There is a spring in my step and a song—many songs—in my heart. I am also in wonder, for I can walk! My step is lighter and more joyous every day.

Thank you for giving me your back when I was alone, ill, vulnerable, and in desperate need of God's mercy and grace. How amazing to be the recipient of one of the miracles that happen every day in this city.

God bless Minneapolis.

Part One

Looking Back

One

Another Look,
and a Second Debridement

October 31, 2007

ℬad, bad, very bad," the physician stated, shaking his head to emphasize how really "bad" it was. I was at the Mayo Medical Center in Rochester, Minnesota, and this was my appointment with the plastic surgeon.

The next day I was scheduled for what is called a debridement—a cleaning—of my right foot, the second in as many months. This appointment was to determine if it was possible to place a flap of skin over an opening on the inside of my right foot to allow the infections that had settled in the bones to drain.

The doctor turned over my appointment sheet, grabbed a pencil, and wrote the names of the infections I carried in huge letters. I already knew I had been diagnosed with a persistent infection status post-debridement of infected talonavicular arthrodesis nonunion, osteomyelitis, and avascular necrosis, but adding MRSA and strep viridans and handing it back to me was more than I was able to take in.

As bad as it was, he was still willing to perform the procedure to drain the infections.

The appointment concluded, I breathed a sigh of relief, got up, stepped on my left foot, and placed the crutches ahead of my right foot, which had either been protected by a walking boot or cast up to the knee, off and on for the last six years.

I got off the elevator to wait for the shuttle to the Super 8 Motel in Rochester, hoping for a good night's rest prior to surgery. At home, I had become used to sleeping with my right foot propped above my heart, but trying to rest in a motel room bed wasn't the same. However, the plastic surgeon's willingness to try cleaning up my foot was enough to relax me just a bit.

By this time, I was in the second round and sixth month of wearing a PICC line that administered medication to my foot. A PICC line (Peripherally Inserted Central Catheter) is a long, slender, small, flexible tube inserted into a peripheral vein, typically in the upper arm, and advanced until the tip of the catheter reaches a large vein above the heart. PICC lines are ordered for a variety of treatment options. In my case, they provided prolonged antibiotic treatment consisting of disposable infusion systems that allowed me to administer 300 mg of antibiotics every 24 hours with an infusion time of 30 minutes for each dose. The thought of possibly getting rid of the PICC line provided enough relief to get me to sleep, though I know I stirred often during the night.

As I checked into the hospital early the next morning, I focused on thoughts of returning home to Glyndon, Minnesota, 325 miles northwest of Rochester, and to my husband, Wayne. Wayne had used up all his vacation, sick, and personal time from work long ago in this difficult journey. I dreaded the long, lonely trips, but perhaps finally all these surgeries would be over.

The debridement was performed late in the day on November 1, 2007, and I didn't return to my hospital room until evening.

Bright and early the next morning, the plastic surgeon, cheery as ever, and a doctor from infectious diseases came into my room and told me the protective flap on the skin on the inside of my foot would be put into place later that day. This was welcome news and I breathed a sigh of relief. Evidently all was good, and finally I would see the end of wearing that hated cast.

Another hour went by and the orthopedic surgeon who had performed the debridement had not yet made his rounds. Although I was anxious to visit with him, I warmed, recalling the plastic surgeon's words, and drifted off to sleep.

My contentment was short-lived. The surgeon walked into my hospital room within the hour. Looking straight ahead, he said, "It's for the best. We'll amputate the foot."

"For the best"?

My ears rang with his words. What on earth did they mean?

Two

Looking Back

How does a baby boomer raised in a small town in North Dakota and living in another small town in western Minnesota end up at the Mayo Clinic hearing "It's for the best" that her right foot be amputated?

I grew up the middle of three children of parents from what Tom Brokaw called "the Greatest Generation." My parents were second-generation Americans of German-Russian descent. I was fortunate to come of age in a community that cared for each other, with parents who saw to it that we were exposed to everything we needed to grow and thrive, including the greatest gifts of all—an abiding faith in God and a good education.

Playing the piano was what I enjoyed most, and my parents sacrificed so that I was able to take lessons from the age of eight through high school. Even today, I never play without holding that knowledge dear to my heart.

I also loved dolls growing up and I haven't quite outgrown that yet, although now I've taken it to a different level—I repair and restore those damaged by the passage of time.

After high school, I began to pursue a degree in piano performance, but that had to be put on hold after I shattered my right femur in an automobile accident. I spent three months in traction, and after undergoing surgery to repair the fracture, three more months in a body cast.

This interrupted my plans, but it didn't touch my sense of mortality or bring a realization that God had different plans for me. I was young. My walk with God wasn't close enough then to be called a walk; it was more of an "I'll check in with you now and then" relationship.

I married young, and several years later, life again took a turn I wasn't planning. We lost an infant son to a rare heart defect and I spun into a deep depression. I didn't yet trust that all things were in God's hands and that He was lovingly watching over me. We were subsequently blessed with two beautiful daughters and had a full, comfortable life, but as our daughters grew, our marriage grew apart. I regret that our daughters had to be the children of divorce; I wish they had been able to experience the safety and security I knew as a child.

For years I continued to work in the legal field as a certified legal assistant. When I remarried and the girls entered adulthood, I decided to return to school to earn a bachelor's degree in business management.

During my time in the business world, an opportunity arose to teach evening classes at a junior college and I decided to give it a try. To my surprise, I found I loved it, and I decided to teach full time. I had found my passion in life, and I enjoyed every moment in the classroom. Life was so good, so comfortable. I couldn't have asked for anything better. I didn't yet know what "letting go and letting God" meant.

Late in 2000, I plantar flexed, or "hyper flexed," my ankle behind my leg in what seemed like a minor misstep when I caught the toe of my shoe on the carpet. It hurt, really hurt, and warranted the attention of a physician.

At his advice, I began a regimen of therapy. The pain remained, so an x-ray was ordered. Nothing stood out, but the pain worsened so a scope was performed. Temporarily, the discomfort eased up just ever so slightly, but then it again escalated. Soon, it seemed no matter what I did, there was discomfort.

Surgical procedures were performed and I began wearing a CAM (Controlled Ankle Motion) walker, a restrictive boot designed to prevent further injury by restricting both voluntary and involuntary movement in the ankle and lower leg. I had further exploratory surgery in 2002 and screws were put into the ankle. At this time, the ankle was first casted. The screws were removed the following year, but I needed surgery again in 2003, again followed by casting the ankle.

I became fatigued but continued teaching. An ankle arthrodesis was performed the following year and again the ankle was casted several times.

When it became too difficult to teach, I requested time off. Still, my foot and ankle swelled and the pain and fatigue didn't lessen so I had further

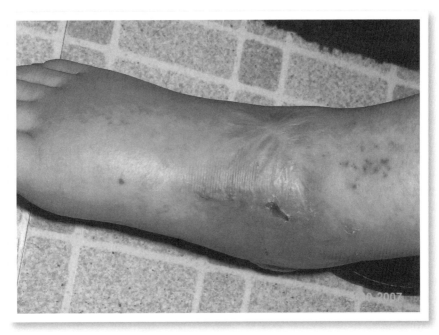

My right foot, September 30, 2007

surgery and casting in 2005. By then, it was no longer possible to be on my ankle any length of time and I had to stop teaching.

Five years after the original accident, I wound up back in the hospital, unable to work, the pain in my ankle and foot unbearable.

Dr. Brent Hella, the attending physician, diagnosed a widespread infection. He ordered my first PICC line, that centrally located catheter that allows antibiotics to be delivered into major blood vessels for extended periods. I wore this for three months, during which time Dr. Hella also recommended that I make an appointment with the Mayo Clinic.

The pain was relentless and I couldn't stand it. Still awaiting word from Mayo—very impatiently as the pain increased and became the primary consideration in every thought and activity—I got into my car and drove to Rochester, alone, in the summer of 2007. I arrived in the ER at St. Mary's Hospital in the wee hours on a Sunday morning.

Within an hour, the orthopedic surgeon arranged for me to see a specialist that following Monday. I did, and the diagnosis was sobering. I had a triple bone infection, including staph, strep viridans, and Methicillin-resistant Staphylococcus aureus, a bacterial infection that is highly resistant to antibiotics. In other words, I had a stubborn, persistent bone infection that was spreading and killing the blood vessels around it.

A procedure was scheduled in which the bones within my foot and ankle were cleaned—my first debridement—and a spacer bar with antibiotic time-released beads was implanted into my foot. This occurred on August 16, 2007. I was fitted with my second PICC line, through which I self-administered medication for nearly three months, which brought me to November 1, 2007.

And so, with the words "It's for the best," the most horrible and yet the most wonderful and humbling part of my life began.

Three
Looking for a Way

As many times as I'd heard the phrase "It's for the best," it had never been about amputating someone's foot, and certainly not mine!

As I lay in my hospital bed, gazing at the physician, I found the silence unbearable and I fought to stay composed. These were just words, and there must be an appropriate way to react, right?

I thought about my dad's sister, my Aunt Marie. What would she do? That composed lady who always knew exactly what to say was not here, and I ached for her wisdom. Everything had suddenly become a blur, and I couldn't speak.

Huge tears rolled down my cheeks. I wanted to ask the doctor to repeat himself, but what I really wanted was to hear him say something else. I waited and hoped my lip would stop shaking. My tears dropped onto the top of my hospital gown and I wiped them away quickly with my arm. I grabbed a tissue—surely that would help—and wiped away the remaining salty water on my face.

No better. Any grogginess remaining from the pain in my leg, the surgical anesthesia, or my brief nap disappeared in a strange flash of light. A dissonant chord resonated throughout my body. I lifted my eyes to see if my foot was still there.

It was, elevated, and covered by a white sheet. Good. I had to check, as if checking would put me in charge of everything.

I was waiting for more words from the doctor. They did not come. The seconds that passed before I could speak seemed like days. I swallowed, pursed my lips as if to "suck it up," and asked, "When?"

"In about three weeks," he said.

There was just too much bone loss to save the foot. The infection had destroyed nearly all the bone in the middle of my foot. The problem, he said, was the location of the infection. Since it was in the middle of my foot, amputating just the infected area wasn't possible.

A procedure called a Symes amputation—the intentional surgical removal of a lower extremity, performed to remove diseased tissue or relieve pain, in my case the entire foot—would have to be done. This was, he repeated, "for the best."

Even though I tried to wrap my mind around what he was saying, I found my thoughts racing. Could we back up and try this again? Wasn't there any way to cut out the bad spots? I'd heard of bad spots being cut out.

I didn't want to hear any of this, but as I watched him, I realized this had to be difficult to say, and I felt sad that he had to be the bearer of such news.

He finished by telling me the healing time after a Symes amputation would be relatively short compared to the debridements I'd had.

By now, I'd had thirteen surgical procedures on this ankle. I allowed myself to think about this ever so briefly. I was getting very weary of the casts, and had gone through the selection of cast colors nearly twice.

The doctor finished his speech and left. Today, I remember the compassion in his voice, but that wasn't what resonated that cold, gray morning.

My thoughts asked questions. What happened to amputated feet? Was there a recycling center for feet? If so, who would get my foot?

Most of all, how would I manage without it?

Four
Looking for Answers

Within twenty-four hours, I'd gone from a short procedure to allow the infection to drain to learning "the best thing" would be to have my foot amputated. I picked away at my breakfast and tried to visualize the word "amputation."

About an hour later, the orthopedic resident came in, placed both hands on the footboard of the bed, and echoed what the surgeon had told me earlier. He, too, was compassionate. He told me just how serious the infections were, and how fast they could spread.

I tried to have a conversation with him about what was coming next. We talked a bit about shoes and my love for them, and he repeated the words the surgeon had spoken earlier in an eerily similar tone of voice, yet I felt his concern and the care with which he stated the word "amputate." He said that after the amputation, I could wear pretty much any style of shoe I wanted and could get back to the business of everyday life.

I honestly can't say I felt better after I talked to him, but my stiff upper lip was in place. I hadn't even called my husband yet. I pushed the button to talk to a nurse, and she very patiently listened as I told her the news.

The staff at Mayo was incredibly kind and each one treated me with the utmost dignity. Even though I hated what was happening, I could tell that these wonderful caregivers did not enjoy having to say this life-changing procedure was necessary. I felt their hearts in their voices, and I knew I would have to call my husband at work if I wanted to talk to him before the end of the day.

I didn't want to tell him at work, but I couldn't wait. I desperately needed to hear his voice. Solid as a rock, he has a calming way about him, and I needed to hear him say everything was going to be okay.

I called him and choked out the words. There was just no way to make them sound matter-of-fact.

He was silent way too long, and I was surprised. Somehow, I'd thought he would be able to do something to prevent this, not just offer me long-distance silence. While I tried to steady my voice, the thought that kept coming was that he would no longer want me around, now a "parts missing" person.

His first question was, "When?"

After I told him, there it was again—silence. Then he told me exactly what I needed to hear. He said he didn't marry me for my foot.

As we hung up, I noticed my ankle was coming back to life from surgery and I practically yelled for something for the discomfort. I remember getting something mild for the pain—I'd gone through the days of strong painkillers and didn't wish to relive them—and went to sleep.

By the time I woke up, it was mid-afternoon. The thought of the coming amputation washed over me like a shooting pain from head to toe. An amputation just did not compute in my head. This foot was my damper pedal foot. It was the foot I kept time to as I learned the French horn. I also used it to play the pedals on the organ. I'd played the organ in church since I was fourteen, and my foot belonged right where it was. There was just too much living left in this foot, and I decided it wasn't going anywhere.

I didn't see the plastic surgeon again for the rest of my hospital stay, which was another three days. I decided all this was a mistake, just a miscommunication among the doctors, but no one returned to inform me that indeed a mistake had been made.

The day before I was released, the resident wheeled in the cart containing all the necessities to cast my foot. He calmly told me about the Symes procedure and how easy it would be for me to heal up and get on with my life. Afterwards, he repeated, I could wear any type of shoe I wanted, as I would be fitted with the proper prosthesis. It would be a mere matter of months before the infection was gone, and I wouldn't have to bother with casts any more.

Somehow, none of this made me feel any better.

Five

Looking for My Ride

November 5, 2007

At 9:00 p.m. on this dark, sub-zero evening, I was wheeled from my hospital room armed with two appointments for November 21, one to remove the stitches from the debridement procedure and the second to meet with physical rehabilitation to get instructions for the care of the stump.

I vaguely remember the nurse wheeling me to the area of the hospital where I would wait for the shuttle that would take me on the approximately hour-long ride to the train station in Winona, Minnesota, where I would catch the Amtrak home.

It was very cold and dark in the waiting area, so dark that it seemed the friendly fellow approached out of nowhere to hesitantly place his hand on the right handle of my wheelchair and ask if I was waiting for a ride to the Amtrak depot. I nodded quickly, fearful there would be competition for space in the shuttle, but no one else responded, and I breathed a sigh of relief.

In a kind, patient tone, he offered to help me board the van. We talked comfortably as we shared work experiences. He practiced law and had the shuttle as a side business.

I found myself momentarily ignoring my plight and enjoying the camaraderie. He was extremely polite, tended to my luggage, and escorted me to another well-mannered person, an Amtrak employee, who told me he would help me "crutch it" to the passenger car.

I sensed he genuinely felt my struggle, and he made his way with a commanding presence through the crowd closely huddled in line against the cold to board the train. The support I received from these two men I now recognize as hope.

The conductor kept a hold on my arm as he reached for a stool, placed it on the ground, and helped me make it up the two steps. It was now about 10:30 p.m., and my head was still ringing with "It's for the best," "It's for the best."

I began to associate the rhythm of the words with a drum cadence, a haunting connection of auditory and visual senses, because it seemed without end and created the tension I remembered similar to the drum beats of the march of the caisson as John F. Kennedy's casket was taken by horses to Arlington Cemetery the day of his funeral in 1963.

How heart-searing it had been! School had been cancelled that dreary November day so long ago, and I recall watching the procession while glued to the black and white TV screen. The resonance was as numbing now as it had been then. I felt I was somehow dishonoring President Kennedy's memory by using it, but it remained with a woefully curious echo.

This was my damper pedal foot; it couldn't be a detached limb.

Six

Looking for Space

November 6, 2007

After the Amtrak employee helped me board the train, I was directed to the section for the physically handicapped. I settled in, silently denying that that particular designation had any relationship with me. There was plenty of room to stretch out my cast, and I was the only passenger in this car. The seat was comfortable, and oh, it felt good to sit down. My mind shifted into a hyper-vigilant mode, as if that would stave off any further thought of amputation. I drifted in and out of an exhausted haze, waking up to see, by turns, a detached foot or a fully healed one. Nothing made sense.

Surfacing in my memory came the recollection of my early teenage years when I began to play the organ for church services. My father very often made it a point when I came home from church to compliment my playing. I remember he sat in "his" chair in the living room, his spot for this time on Sunday mornings. Almost as soon as I walked in the door, still taking my coat off and hanging it in the hall closet, he would say, "You really played well today," or "Was that music great to listen to this morning."

Many times, I had made numerous mistakes and I knew he knew it, but I also knew it was going to be all right because his comments were always positive. I didn't realize until years later just how important and fortifying these comments were. They provided the hope I needed to keep going. I recall him saying one Sunday morning during this exchange, "To whom much is given, much is expected."

I hope and pray that I have heeded his words and that he would be proud to know I took them to heart. I intend to play as long as I can, and I will cherish his encouragement forever.

When the train stopped in Minneapolis at 12:10 a.m., a man boarded. His voice was raspy and I could tell, even through my incredible self-absorption, that he was tired and really needed to sit and rest. I squinted to see him more clearly. He walked with a cane, struggling to get on. His conversation with the Amtrak employee pleasantly distracted me. I welcomed this distraction, hoping it would last long enough for this nightmare to be over, but for a brief second, I also resented his intrusion into what I decided was "my" space. I had decided to claim rights to this section even though I wouldn't own its designation. In my mind, the aisles were simply wider, making it possible for anyone to move about with little or no difficulty.

The man's voice, deep and soothing, niggled at my conscience. He came toward me and sat down in the aisle seat directly across from me. I gathered my coat and wrapped it around me like a blanket and tried to settle into a semi-reclining position, certain that somehow he would see my importance and offer silence so I wouldn't have to deal with him. He turned his face toward me, but all I could make out was a silhouette. He nodded in the direction of my elevated foot and asked if I minded sharing the circumstances.

Although I said no, I really did mind, and I hoped the tone of my voice might discourage him. I was not ready in any way to speak of an impending amputation. Instead, I briefly explained how I had struggled with this foot for seven years and thirteen surgeries following a simple turn of my ankle.

His silence was compassionate, and I could sense his concern by the way he leaned his head closer toward me, even though I still could not see his face in the darkness. I had resented his presence at first, but suddenly I felt myself overwhelmed by a sense of calm and I yearned for him to speak, too.

He started telling me about his medical history and struggles with his own foot, and I was glad to have a connection with someone who had experienced a similar struggle. He told me he'd also been close to having his foot amputated, but on the advice of a stranger, he had talked to a surgeon. Today, even though he walked with a cane, he had his foot.

He got my attention, this person I still could not see. I had never heard a voice so calm. His boarding in downtown Minneapolis, I realized, was no accident. He told me of his faith journey, and I was amazed at the peaceful tone in his voice. Even though my faith was foremost in my mind from the time he boarded—no coincidence either—I still didn't want to contemplate how I could ever thank God for the loss of my foot. I had been trying to figure out how losing a limb could be to the glory of God, and the belief of knowing His plan is perfect just wasn't making sense. As was the norm, I prayed that the reason for all of this would become clear to me *now*, and that it would somehow take care of all of my doubts and fears.

At that moment, the stranger offered me a Bible. He told me that he always carried two, because every time he traveled to the VA Hospital in Minneapolis, which was often, or anywhere else, he consistently struck up a conversation with someone and always was convicted to share God's promises with one who needed the comfort of the Word. He said someone was always in need of a Bible. He told me how blessed he was to be able to pass on that everything and the only thing necessary was in that book. It would give me the answers I was so desperately seeking, he told me, and his voice revealed his wish to offer comfort when life "didn't make sense."

He said that after spending many, many hours in the Word, he felt the "peace that passeth all understanding." He said that when he finally "let go," God's peace came to him. This was something he'd never experienced before, and it was there for me as well, if only I would open my heart and seek it.

He also told me the name of the doctor who had finally been able to save his foot, although he attributed this to nothing short of a miracle. He asked if he might pray for me, and the tears came so easily. I wiped them away with my coat. It was such a relief to be able to cry. It was absolutely pitch dark, and I hadn't yet cried over the news.

It seemed like just an hour had passed, but when we reached Fargo, it was already nearly 6:00 a.m. I called my husband and told him I was waiting at the Amtrak depot. I told this stranger, whose face glowed with assurance when I finally saw it as we entered the depot, that we could give him a ride home. He said no, he was accustomed to calling a cab.

I told him absolutely not, that we'd be happy to take him to his home, and he reluctantly agreed. When Wayne arrived, this man, who didn't seem like a stranger anymore, got into the back seat of the car and was very quiet the few short miles to his home. He quickly shut the car door and left in a bit of a run, due to the below zero damp night air. He never offered his name, but I remember the soft-spoken voice that returned the word "Thanks" and the bright, almost glowing, smile that lingered in the air and hung in the falling snow as he disappeared quickly under the two street lights, dimmed by the slight wind pushing the snow on that early November morning.

This stranger who was on his way home from Minneapolis didn't just "coincidentally" board the train in Minneapolis. He was the first of many summoned to watch over me while I traveled from place to place in that city, but it will always escape me that I wasn't aware and thankful that he was the angel who started the procession of thousands to come and touch me with God's love as I began this journey. One reason may be because he was not from Minneapolis, or perhaps I just needed way, way more humbling before I could connect the dots and drop to my knees as if to faint, struck even today with such awe that God cared for me in a way that will always bring tears of joy.

That train ride home was only the beginning of "keeping company with angels."

Seven

Where Do I Begin to Look?

November 6, 2007

I spent the next several weeks on the phone and the Internet, trying to digest the news.

I continued to hover between denial and acceptance of even needing treatment beyond just another surgical procedure. I still thought it was a mistake and that someone would call or write and everything would stay just as it was, just as I thought it should be.

My sister and brother phoned, genuinely concerned. Neither of my parents were living and I needed the sweet comfort of those voices with whom I'd grown up. Although neither had a solution, it was ever so soothing to know they cared, and I'll always recall the compassion of their voices in my heart.

Four years had passed since I'd lost my mother, and they had been tough. Mom and I had been quite close, but she'd developed dementia in her last years and I wasn't able to spend much time with her because of my foot.

Had she been alive, she would have been just a phone call away and would have known what to say in her matter-of-fact way. I believed she would have known another way to resolve this and that she would tell me it was just a minor bump in the road, though perhaps a bit more challenging than other bumps. I also thought about how many times, when talking about life's difficulties, she would tell us to imagine a group of people sitting in a circle throwing all their problems in the middle. She had always emphasized that each would take their own problems back because they knew how to manage them. I tried to rely upon the strength of her faith, and the memory of the comfort she would have offered.

Eight
Looking and Listening

November 12, 2007

Monday evening, three days after my arrival home, Pastor Rick Larson and his wife Carol stopped by with a pizza for supper. Somehow they are always there at the right time. Wayne and I shared the news with them, and for the first time, I sobbed. My vulnerability surfaced, and we spent a lot of time in prayer, both silent and aloud. Choking out the news to them was the first time it really, really was driven home—at home.

Throughout the next three weeks, waiting for what now seemed inevitable, I had a lot of time to reflect. I recalled an appointment in October at Mayo in which a Symes amputation had been discussed. I had forgotten this had even been a consideration. It seemed as though the fate of my foot was sealed.

Because of my foot, I had been unable to work for several years, so I had begun volunteering at the Dakota Boys and Girls Ranch thrift store in Moorhead. Although I wanted to maintain a regular schedule, between clinic appointments, emergency room visits, and just plain not being able to stand for very long, I suspect I was more of a hindrance than a help. When I did work, it was for short periods of time and very sporadically.

Hannah, the assistant manager, and Lisa, the manager, and the rest of the staff were such good listeners. As time went by and my challenges with my foot continued, they displayed genuine compassion.

While I likely rambled on incessantly, in retrospect, I think they too are angels. The stranger who had boarded the train in downtown Minneapolis had renewed my strength; now I wanted to learn anything and everything I could whenever and wherever I could. I found a captive and caring audience at this place and with these people who largely represented my social life, and I was eager to hear anything that might stave off this amputation.

I recalled a discussion with Hannah about oxygen treatments her husband had received for heart trouble at the Whitaker Wellness Institute in California, but in no way did I connect that to my condition.

When I called my mother-in-law, the comfort of her voice caused me to fully break down. She listened as all my fears came out and kept telling me, "Do not give up." Her voice was full of faith and love. She absolutely would not give up believing that something could save this foot I had struggled so long to keep.

During the next three weeks, I spoke with her for many hours, working my way through the grieving process. She was always there to listen, to comfort, and to tell me she believed something could and would be done other than amputation.

Little does she know how I cherish her as though she was my own mother; she has the wonderful gift of wisdom and a no-nonsense yet caring way of stating things that just makes sense and offers a comfort that alleviates anxiety. I called her so often, and I know where I was sitting the day she lit the spark of hope brightly in my soul and gave me the strength to really, really believe that I would be able to find a way to save my foot.

Nine
Taking a Hard Look

November 21, 2007

Wayne and I took off early on a cold, overcast morning for the dreaded six-hour drive from our home in Glyndon, Minnesota, to Rochester. It was time to see the surgeon again, and time to make arrangements for the amputation. We exchanged few words, each of us enveloped in our own vision of the future. We both liked the upbeat music of the 1950s, and we were relieved the radio station played some of our favorites. I welcomed the distraction because I didn't want to burden Wayne with my fears. It was all getting too close and too real.

A "shoo-bop" song started, reminding me of the time we entered and won a jitterbug contest many years before. The doctor's confident "It's for the best" still stung my brain, and I took many, many deep breaths during this long ride. I wanted to slow our arrival, but I also longed to see the doctor, hoping he had changed his mind.

When we arrived at the hospital, my husband quickly found a wheelchair. We registered, put on surgical gowns, and waited for my name to be called. I had to switch from the wheelchair to a hospital bed and I didn't like that at all. The cast came off and we waited.

The doctor and the resident came into the room and I gulped, knowing as their eyes met mine that there wasn't going to be any change of mind. The doctor talked again about the amputation. He removed the stitches, told the nurses to put my leg back in a cast, and told us to proceed to physical therapy, where I would learn how to take care of the stump.

I froze, and deliberately tuned all the voices to mute. I sat as though I appeared to be engaged in this serious, life-changing discussion, but I still did not believe it was really me they were talking about—it must have been some other Jean Mahlum at another time and place.

Finally, I asked if there were any other options. Vaguely recalling my conversation with Hannah about her husband's oxygen therapy, I mentioned that. Of course her husband's circumstances were different, but I was grabbing for anything I could think of.

Both doctors were very skeptical about the use of oxygen in my case. They didn't believe it would be useful, and there wasn't anything else they could try.

I looked at my husband and told him I didn't want to keep the appointment in physical therapy. To me, keeping that appointment meant signing my foot away.

He very calmly told me we would just hear what they had to say—it didn't necessarily mean there were no other options and we weren't going to stop looking for them.

So, as he insisted we press on, he again found a wheelchair and we headed off toward the clinic, a long silent journey. I noticed his pace slowed the nearer we came to the appointment desk. When my name was called, we went into a room where we were joined by two doctors and a physical therapist. There we were, the five of us. I dropped my head into my hands and closed my eyes. Briefly, I attempted to put on the appearance of someone who was looking on rather than being the focus of this discussion.

They proceeded to show me pictures of what my stump would look like and it was as though someone was flipping pages of a show and tell booklet. The narrator slowly explained the procedure; I believe he knew how difficult it was to hear these words. I simply had to dissociate. There just was not, could not, be an amputation.

I heard someone in my head say, "Wait a minute; you're way too young to have your foot amputated. You have no heart problems, no diabetes, no respiratory problems, or other health problems, and you're about thirty years too young to be facing losing a limb."

Exactly! I couldn't have agreed more. However, there simply was no other way for the foot to heal. This was the day before Thanksgiving, and the best time for the procedure was in approximately one week.

They seemed to talk about it so casually, like ordering a meal in a restaurant. Though I now recall the compassion in their voices, what they were saying wasn't what I wanted to hear, and I couldn't think beyond that.

After the appointments, we headed for the parking ramp, neither of us saying anything about what had just taken place. Instead, we turned our attention and conversation to the neutral topic of the weather and how cold it was. We asked each other, exactly at the same time, where the car was parked. It wasn't long before we found it, since we both remembered. We got in and started home. For a while, neither of us spoke.

On the drive home, Wayne raised the question about insurance coverage for amputations and whether or not I had ever read about such coverage. Of course I hadn't; he knew it and so did I. I think we both just needed to be able to say the word aloud.

Without further comment, I called our health insurance company. Because I was considered a "complicated case" by now, I had my own nurse, Kathy Kennedy, who was so patient as she talked to me on the phone over and over for months.

I told her about the latest developments and she was silent a long time. I asked her what else could be done and she asked if I knew anything about hyperbaric medicine.

I said no, and she explained that she had recently heard about its various uses for medical conditions and she believed there might be a facility in Minneapolis that offered this "diving medicine."

I still felt as though I was someone else on the outside looking in. After we finished speaking, I told my husband what she'd said. Neither of us had a clue as to how this might relate to my condition, but we decided we'd somehow find out.

There was very little power left on my cell phone and I had no car charger, but I called information to get the number of the Minneapolis Chamber of Commerce. Hopefully they would be able to direct me to this facility that offered hyperbaric oxygen treatment. I got the number, but my phone lost power.

Suddenly, so did I. I sat in silence the rest of the trip home. It was sub-zero weather and overcast, and the tears once again rolled down my cheeks.

At this point, I said, "I give up."

Wayne said, "No, because you won't be able to hold your granddaughter's hand and go for a walk in the backyard."

Ten

Looking for Peace

November 22, 2007

I sat up until 2:00 a.m. just trying to think, leafing through the Bible given to me by the man on the train. I prayed the words would just jump out at me, that healing would take place, with no further effort on my part. One particular page of the Bible I had received at my confirmation came to mind. My grandma had underlined her favorite verse in that Bible, Matthew 6:33: "Seek ye first the Kingdom of God and His righteousness and all these things shall be added unto you."

The reassuring voice of my grandma saying those words made me close my eyes with a relief that washed over me. I hadn't remembered the sweet sound of her voice in many years, and it was now absolutely crystal clear and comforting. This is a precious, precious memory. Grandma was so kind; whenever she received candy, she would open the box and immediately offer the first piece to the person who had given it to her, saying, "Love the giver." I've never heard of anyone else doing that, and I thought of how rare it must have been that she received candy, and how I probably would have gone for the biggest piece right away without even considering sharing it first.

My self-pity needed to go. Finally, I prayed to accept whatever was to be, not what I thought was "for the best," but what was truly "for the best" in transforming my life, in making me an instrument for His will.

I tried to visualize exactly what being a "light" was. I recalled a play on words my Uncle Milton once told me about the hymn "I Surrender All." He said it was easier to call it "I Surrender Some." I had to agree. I cherish the conversations we had, brief as they were, because I loved the way he talked. He had such faith and conviction and was passionate about life and his faith. I remember him elaborating about how hard we hang on to things and worry until we're exhausted before we remember to look up and hand over the heavy, heavy burdens to Him and let Him be the driver.

The next morning was Thanksgiving. Somehow, I felt a renewed sense of calm and peace. Even though I couldn't speak to anyone at the Minneapolis Chamber of Commerce that day, I was content to wait until the next day. That's how far God had taken me in such a short time. To have the patience to wait until Friday morning was, for me, just touching the surface of "the peace that passeth understanding" that I had never once experienced in all my fifty-five years.

My husband and I gave thanks for each other on this day. We prepared a small turkey roll that came in its own gravy, cooked carrots, and gave thanks for all we had, and the meal nourished us in body and soul. It was a good day, and God rewarded us with a renewed strength and determination to keep on, even though we didn't have any answers, much less know any of the questions.

I didn't know how worried Wayne was at that time; in fact, I didn't know for many months to come.

Eleven

Please Take a Look

November 23, 2007

Friday morning, the day after Thanksgiving, I got up bright and early with a renewed sense of energy, called the Minneapolis Chamber of Commerce, and got the numbers of all the hospitals in Minneapolis. The only reason I can imagine that I didn't use the Internet was that I believed voice-to-voice contact would better the chances that someone would be inclined to help me. Perhaps if someone heard desperation in my voice, I would be directed to what I was looking for.

It was nearly 3:00 p.m. before I had all the information I needed to start forming a plan. In retrospect, I was held up and fortified by Him, not knowing it was His plan all along. I thought I was in charge. I am just amazed at how clueless I was, but I know now that it was only because of His plan that I could plan anything.

I learned that Hennepin General was the home of the Hennepin County Trauma Center, where hyperbaric oxygen therapy was used to treat various conditions.

I still didn't know what "hyperbaric" meant. All I knew was that divers with "the bends" received oxygen therapy, as did victims of carbon monoxide poisoning, and I didn't fit either category.

Barb Elkins, the patient representative at the Hennepin County Medical Center, was very kind. She transferred me to the Hennepin County Hyperbaric Chamber (HCHC) and a person named Ginny, the most awesome nurse in the world, answered the phone in such a cheery voice that I've never forgotten it. I told her my situation and she said they needed more information and she would talk to the director of the trauma center.

Within half an hour, Dr. Cher Adkinson called me back. She said they would have to see me, and there was only one available time—Wednesday, November 28, the same day I was supposed to return to Mayo for the amputation of my foot. If I wanted a place in the Hennepin County Hyperbaric Chamber, I would have to come as soon as possible to consult with the physician in charge of admitting.

As we spoke, the words "chronic, refractory osteomyelitis" stood out. I recalled seeing them on Dr. Kitaoka's discharge summary following the most recent surgery and the phrase took on a rhythm of its own and went back and forth in my head like a ping-pong ball. Would I be there for that 1:00 p.m. appointment? There was no doubt about it.

The doctor explained that hyperbaric treatment would take months, at least forty-plus treatments, with no guarantee it would work, but she agreed to set up the initial appointment. She gave me directions to the trauma center and we said goodbye.

I had absolutely no idea what to expect. Ginny told me I would have to stay in Minneapolis for the treatments, so I spoke again with Barb Elkins. Helpfully, she told me about living quarters available for long-term outpatients, and we decided the only option was to stay in a motel close enough to downtown that I could take a shuttle to the hyperbaric chamber. I was in no condition to walk, even half a city block, nor could I drive or even take the city bus. I would have to stay somewhere that furnished transportation and allowed me to stay by the month.

The following Wednesday found us back on the road to Minneapolis, weary yet eager. Little did I know that I was in for a profound, life-changing five months.

Twelve

We'll Take a Look at It

November 28, 2007

The trauma center in downtown Minneapolis is located in a small building behind a small parking lot. There is no parking lot for the staff or patients at the trauma center; it's simply a "drive-in, drop-off, and pick up" entry. After circling the block at least three or four times, we found a parking lot about two blocks away with half-day parking. Although two blocks away was not "nearby" to me in the shape I was in, I was eager to head out on my crutches and find out more about this place, and I kept up with my husband's stride.

The small building was not easy to find. It was very cold outside, and I was unaccustomed to walking outdoors, but I was eager to hear what they had to say. Positive thoughts and a feeling of calm swept over me as we entered a small waiting room.

The first thing I noticed was the smell of freshly brewed coffee. I remember the full waiting room, all the folks chatting. Everyone seemed to know each other by name, and their concern for one another was remarkable. This was not a scene I was used to seeing in a medical waiting room.

The person behind the desk said, "You must be Jean. We've been waiting for you. Please have a seat and we'll call you back as soon as we can."

I was relieved; they hadn't changed their mind about the consultation.

I met a number of staff members and saw the hyperbaric chamber, which was huge, like a steel igloo. I got a big smile and a warm greeting from Ginny, the nurse I had spoken to on the phone. She took me to the examination area where I met Dr. Robert Collier, who explained how hyperbaric oxygen therapy works.

Even though my first impression of the chamber was that of an igloo, it actually looked more like a submarine. Hennepin County Medical Center's is a multi-place chamber, which means several patients can receive treatment at once.

Hyperbaric oxygen therapy, I learned, dissolves high concentrations of oxygen into the blood and tissues. Certain types of infections, tissue injuries, and poisonings can be treated effectively if the body is saturated regularly with oxygen in this way. The extra oxygen can help heal wounds and fight infections.

Inside the chamber, the air contains two-and-a-half times the amount of oxygen in the atmosphere. This pressure on the outside of the body allows more oxygen to get to the bloodstream and build more blood vessels, which increases circulation to infections or wounds.

The treatment is commonly called "diving medicine" because the atmospheric pressure is the equivalent of 46 feet below sea level. You stay in the chamber for 110 minutes, breathing 100% pure oxygen through a facemask for ninety minutes. The rest of the time is for compression and decompression of the chamber.

Hyperbaric oxygen therapy patients are generally treated once a day, some twice a day; the number of treatments and the duration and exact pressure used depends on the patient's condition.

After a lengthy exam, Dr. Collier told me they would give it a try.

There were no sweeter words he, or anyone, could have said. He did tell me it was going to be a long road and he wanted to know if I was ready for that.

Ready? I wanted to start that day!

There was just one catch. I needed a referral, and I was afraid that was impossible. When I'd last seen the physicians at Mayo, they'd told me there was no use in trying hyperbaric treatments, so a referral was not going to come from them. I had told my physician in Fargo what Mayo's opinion was and he'd agreed, so now what?

Dr. Collier leaned back against the wall, crossed his arms, took a long look at me, and then turned his gaze toward the window. He said, "Well, you can be a self-referral."

Yes, yes, yes! They were willing to give it a shot, and I was in!

I was told how the procedure worked. Each day, I would arrive before 8:00 a.m. and undergo a medical assessment to determine if there had been any changes in my condition within the previous twenty-four hours.

Then I would change into a cotton shirt and slacks and slip into disposable booties. Once in the chamber, I would sit in a reclining chair, like those in a dental office. I would be grounded to a wire and given a blanket, since the chamber was somewhat cold as we "came up" from the "dive."

After everyone was readied, the chamber would be sealed and we would begin the dive. If everyone tolerated the compression well, we would be given facemasks to breathe pure oxygen for ninety minutes. The extra twenty minutes allowed for the "diving down" and "coming up," the expressions the technicians used to describe the chamber compressing and decompressing.

In the end, I didn't need a self-referral after all. Thanks to Dr. Brent Hella of Internal Medicine Associates in Fargo, the doctor who was my attending physician at the ER at the local hospital the last time I needed medical attention prior to going to Mayo, I became a referred patient at the Hennepin County Hyperbaric Chamber. I owe thanks to my doctor and the staff at Mayo, who sent my medical records. No one at the Hennepin County Hyperbaric Chamber had seen my foot because it was in a cast, so my records were all they had to go on.

After approximately three hours at the facility, we were ready to go to the motel that would be my home for the greater part of the next five months. That day, I became a resident of Minneapolis. The remarkable thing about living there was that I can recall fewer than a handful of times when I hobbled up to the entrance of a public place and someone did not open the door for me. Nor did any person who waited on me fail to say, whether or not they asked about my big cast and crutches, either "God bless you" or "I'll pray for you."

That is a miracle.

Hennepin County Hyperbaric Chamber Control Panel, November 2007

Entrance to Hyperbaric Chamber No. 3, November 2007

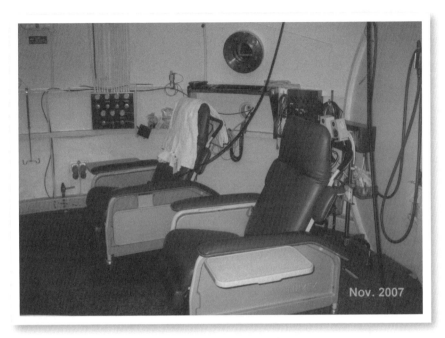

Inside Hyperbaric Chamber No.3, patient seats, November 2007

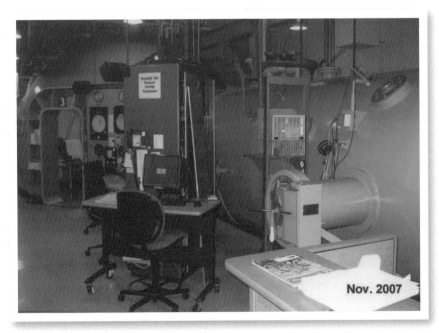

View outside Hennepin County Hyperbaric Chamber, November 2007

Thirteen
Looking at Moving In

My new home was Room 517 at the Days Inn University in Minneapolis. All I brought was one large suitcase. There hadn't been much time to gather my belongings, and we didn't have much to move in. The cast on my right leg prevented me from being able to wear many of my slacks, and I had resorted to just three—two pairs of sweatpants whose middle seam I had slit just enough to cover my cast and one pair of faded jeans that I had slit as well. I also had several t-shirts, two sweaters, a sweatshirt, a pair of pajamas, and three pairs of socks and underwear. I'd also brought the flour sack dishtowels on which I had ironed transfers I wanted to embroider for Christmas gifts.

Suitcase deposited, my husband and I took on the arduous task of buying food and whatever else I might need to sustain me for a month, as he wouldn't be able to return to Minneapolis until Christmas. I would not be able to get out to restaurants or grocery stores, so we needed to make certain I was well supplied. I was going to be on my own, and I wouldn't be able to run out and grab something at the last minute.

List-making is not my strength, but Wayne is very organized. He compiled a comprehensive list and thought of everything. He asked me which microwavable dishes I would like, what soup I would like, what I wanted to drink, and what kind of snacks I would like.

My mind was so full of everything that had happened that day that I wasn't hungry or even thinking about food. I was so excited to be starting oxygen treatments that nothing else seemed to matter, but Wayne was serious and continued to insist that I needed to be sure I had enough to eat.

We spent a great deal of time at Wal-Mart, going aisle to aisle stocking up on items such as peanut butter, jelly, jam, Oreos, crackers, and plastic knives, forks, and spoons, patiently marking off all the items on his list.

I still didn't know what I was getting into. I didn't know what I would be doing during my "off" time, other than lying on my back with my foot propped up above my heart on a foam cushion my husband had made, and I had no idea how many hours each day oxygen treatments would take. All I knew was that I was to receive the first treatment tomorrow, November 29, and I would have to be at the trauma center before 8:00 a.m.

Wayne stayed overnight with me in my new home and helped put everything away. He was exhausted and fell asleep before 10:00 p.m., but I had a great deal of difficulty dropping off. I was unable to properly place the covers on top of my right leg as it lay propped above my heart. I had become somewhat accustomed to doing this at home, but I wasn't used to this bed and the covers felt uncomfortably heavy on my foot.

Finally, I went to sleep thinking what a snap it was going to be to have the first treatment, and how I would feel so much better—I fervently hoped—the next day.

Fourteen
Looking the Other Way

November 29, 2007

My husband was up early, listening to the weather on TV. The temperature was zero degrees. He opened the drapes and started his car with his automatic starter. He needed to get an early start. Not only was he having some problems with his car that had already logged so many miles transporting me for medical attention, he needed to get back to work, and he wasn't eager to face the possibility of dealing with a stalled car in -20 degree weather on the long trip back home.

I wanted to get that last glance of him pulling out of the parking lot, but I had to look away. It was simply too painful to watch him leave, so I crawled back into bed, knowing I had to be in the lobby before 7:30 a.m. in order to make my first treatment.

A little while later, up and dressed, I stopped at the second floor hospitality room for a continental breakfast. Upon entering the room, I was amazed to see a petite woman handling boxes of doughnuts and other food with ease. At this point, I hardly had the strength to get around.

I was trying to add hot water to instant oatmeal when I heard a voice behind me asking if I needed help. I thought I could do it myself, but I stumbled and quickly caught myself just before I dumped the bowl.

I accepted her help and asked for a banana. It was getting late, and I had to hurry to make the shuttle. She offered to help me clean up, and I thanked her and headed toward the elevator.

Don, the Days Inn shuttle driver, was waiting at the front desk. As he walked toward the door, people started to follow. He went to the driver's door, brought a foot stool around to the front passenger seat, and helped me board. This very kind man did this every time he drove the shuttle, ever so patiently. It was two steps up and they were quite high and he never hesitated to help me, nor did he ever rush me. I thanked him each time, and he always told me it was nothing.

Everyone else boarded and off we went. Don had been at this a while, and I was amazed at how he worked his way through the downtown traffic during the early morning rush. The motel shuttle transported guests within a two-mile radius, the exact distance to the trauma center. I would be the last passenger off because I had the farthest to go. When we arrived, he brought the stool around and carefully helped me out and into the center.

I was greeted with bright smiles and told to come toward the chamber, where I received a brief exam and was handed the requisite cotton top, slacks, and booties. As soon as I changed, I was ready for the procedure. I just had no idea what to expect.

Fifteen

Looking around the Chamber

Once we were all seated in the chamber, given water to drink, and tucked in our blankets, the words came through the microphone: "Are you ready to dive?"

What I heard was "Are you ready to DIE?" I panicked, and thought, oh, oh, this all had been a dream too good to be true, and immediately tried to rise out of my chair. The person beside me asked what was wrong, and I told her. She said, "Oh, no, dear, are you ready to DIVE?" Whew! It wasn't a dream—I could relax; I took my seat again; relieved and ready to dive!

The nurse looked at all of us before she responded "Yes," and so it began.

I heard the rush of air and my ears began to pop. I swallowed several times. I now understood why the staff passed out sticks of gum before the treatments began. Chewing gum helped to ease the pressure in the chamber, which was similar to the sensation of the pressure change during an airline flight. My ears began popping like crazy and the temperature change in the chamber was definitely noticeable. I appreciated the thermal blanket I was huddled under.

It was serious business inside this chamber. We could not wear our watches because the glass could burst. Our reading material had to be resistant to the compression, and we could not use Styrofoam cups to hold water because they would melt.

43

The process lasted approximately two hours. We had breaks on the half-hour and were always asked how we were doing before continuing. I don't recall the oxygen having a particular taste or odor, just that it was very refreshing

As time went on, I looked forward to the treatments. When the treatment time elapsed, we were asked, "Are you ready to come up?" Always, my ears popped many times. I learned this was normal, my body adjusting to the atmosphere. I remember feeling almost euphoric after each treatment, and very energized. With that came a voracious appetite, as though I had spent all day outside breathing fresh air.

At the beginning, there was a slight fatigue. As that dissipated, I began to feel better and better each day. Painless and energizing, this was the beginning of a very, very positive experience.

Sixteen
Look What I Got!

I had been in Minneapolis less than a week and had undergone three treatments when I returned to my room to find a message on my phone. It was from my dear Uncle Frank, who offered cheer and a new joke every time we spoke. Hearing his chuckle kept me going and I quickly returned his call.

He had heard about my foot and wanted to know what he could do. Very curious about the hyperbaric chamber, he told me that at the University of Montana, one of the instructors had devoted his attention to finding an antigen for the infections I had. He spoke of a physician who'd used the procedure with diabetic patients and had 90% success in saving their limbs rather than amputating them. I was eager to get this information, and he said he would send it that day.

Uncle Frank called me nearly every day in Minneapolis. We've stayed very close, and I am exceedingly grateful for the support he and Aunt Peg gave me. It has created a bond like no other. My father went to his heavenly home in 1990, and from that time on I've looked to Uncle Frank for the wisdom of my dad. They were so much alike that it warms my heart to visit with him, and I thank God every day for Uncle Frank and his family; he'll never know how much his support meant to me. I knew no one in downtown Minneapolis, and he offered me company, comfort, and hope at a time when I needed it most. Most of all, he made me laugh.

Picture with message "Never Give Up" received from Uncle Frank, December 6, 2007

I also received a package less than a week after I was in Minneapolis wrapped in Christmas paper. Wow! Someone had remembered me!

I opened it slowly, so grateful to receive a present that I wanted to make the moment last, and found a wooden wall hanging of the word "Believe" from my husband's sister. I began to cry and placed it on the stand above the television.

That same day, I received an envelope from Uncle Frank. In it was the second of the two visuals that kept me going during this lonely time away from Wayne. I taped Uncle Frank's "Never Give Up" cartoon by the TV next to the "Believe" hanging, and when I woke up each morning, these were the first things I saw.

I began to settle into a routine: pick up the phone receiver at the wake-up call at 6:30 a.m., grab my crutches, and make my way to the bathtub. Place the shower sleeve on my cast, shower, and limp to my clothes hanging near the bathroom. Get dressed, brush my teeth, and do my hair.

I was always tired by the time I reached the second floor for breakfast, and I worried every day that I would miss the shuttle, or that the shuttle would be too full and I would miss a treatment.

Toward the end of the first week, I noticed that even though this year was unusually overcast, I hadn't experienced the symptoms of seasonal affective disorder (SAD) that I had struggled with for fourteen years. I began to wonder if it was just the concentration on making it day-to-day, or if the oxygen had energized me. Either way, this was a relief.

Seventeen

Looking at Others

My room had a view. The window faced southeast, and the motel was near a large parking lot. However, it was the sight next to the parking lot that stays with me. It was a large building that might have been an office or business of some kind, but its many windows were no longer in place. It looked as though it was ready to be razed. I never saw any lights on, but I saw people walking inside the building nearly every day.

Since there was neither power nor windows, I didn't understand why they went there, but within days I figured it out. In these below-normal temperatures, homeless people were seeking shelter.

I knew this life existed, but as long as I didn't ever see people living in such conditions, I never thought about them. Yet there they were, looking, I'm sure, not only at the Days Inn, but everywhere else that was truly "shelter."

Seeing these homeless people awakened something in me I was not very comfortable with. That evening, I looked down at the new carpet on the floor in Room 517 and counted my blessings. Taking up residence here was going to change the way I looked at many things.

I also noticed the majority of the women who worked in housekeeping wore beautiful long skirts and had their heads covered. I didn't like the fact that whenever I saw them, they either looked down or away. I hoped it wasn't something in my eyes that made them avert theirs.

The majority of those working in housekeeping and maintenance were in their mid-twenties to early thirties and all were hard workers. As the weeks went by, I developed relationships with them that I am proud to say I have sustained to this day. Every person who worked at this motel treated me with the utmost respect, kindness, and compassion. They anticipated my needs and went out of their way to make certain I was comfortable and did not struggle. I thank God for the opportunity to meet them.

Early in my stay, I lost one of the diamond earrings my husband had given me. Since it was a post earring, I didn't think the chances of finding it were very good. I left a note on the desk, asking the person in charge of cleaning my room to take a look if she had time. When I returned, there it was, attached to a piece of paper, lying on the bed. Unbelievable!

It is impossible for me to name all the things my new friends did for me, from finding me ink pens, safety pins, and band-aids to sharing pizza with me when they ordered in to giving me hugs every time I saw them in the hall. Every time I saw an employee, I was warmly greeted, asked how I was doing, and whether or not I needed assistance with anything. This was a surprise, and far beyond any customer service I had ever seen. These people were, and are, a blessing in my life.

Part Two
Looking Deep Within

Eighteen
Looking at Being Thankful

Sleep had been difficult for me for the greater part of the past three years. To have my leg propped above my heart meant I had to sleep on my back without changing position. In retrospect, I believe I was very sleep-deprived, but I was so focused on trying to get out of that cast that I didn't think about it.

As the days went on, I found I wasn't resting well. Lying flat on my back was not my position of choice, and I decided to call my doctor and see if there was anything I could do or some medication I could take to help me sleep.

My call was promptly returned, and I was asked where I would like to have the prescription filled. I requested the nearby Wal-Mart where Wayne and I had bought my supplies. Unfortunately, it was outside the shuttle's range, so I would have to take the city bus.

More than two feet of snow was on the ground, and it had been coming so fast the snowplows couldn't keep up. The pedestrian crossings were snow- and ice-compacted, not exactly ideal for someone on crutches with exposed toes on one foot, but I really, really needed to get some sleep, so I set out for the bus stop.

By the time I boarded the bus, I was exhausted. Anxiously, I asked the driver to please point out the closest stop to Wal-Mart so I didn't have to walk too far. She smiled and said "Sure."

When she stopped, I looked at the snow between the street and the sidewalk and decided it wasn't going to get any better than this.

I got off, tried to feel my way in the hard snow for tracks, and fell down. I got up, determined to make the half-block walk that now looked at least twice that far. It was very chilly, and my coat and gloves didn't warm me.

Once in the store, the greeter asked how she could help. Before I could say anything, she told me there was only one motorized cart in the place and it was being recharged. I thanked her and made my slow way to the pharmacy. It was mid-afternoon, only two Saturdays before Christmas, and the place was packed.

By the time I made it to the pharmacy window, I was ready to collapse. I made my purchase and slowly moved my way through the crowd toward the front of the store, back to the bus stop. That's when I heard a voice beside me. I glanced left, sensing someone needed to get around me. I thought what a good idea it would be to have a "slow-moving vehicle" sign pinned to my back. The day was getting very long, and I figured I would probably take another tumble in the snow before nightfall.

I looked left again and caught the glance of a woman with warm brown eyes. She leaned over and spoke in a very soft voice that I strained to hear. In a voice filled with such concern and genuine inquisitiveness that I was drawn to her, she repeated, "May I help you with something?" Again, I noticed the warmth in her eyes.

Filled with gratitude, I began to tear up. I told her I was doing all right, thanked her for asking, and said I was headed for the bus stop. I glanced ahead, weary but determined. It was going to take a while to get there, and it was below zero outside.

This same woman slowed to my pace, and said, "Would you like to come over for supper?"

Astonished, I remember thinking she had to be kidding.

She told me it was going to be a birthday supper for a young man, nothing special, but she'd like it very much if I could make it.

I thought by then that I would die right here in Wal-Mart in downtown Minneapolis anyway, so why not? I told her yes, but that I didn't want to bother her. She said it was no bother, to just wait by the door, and she would pull her car up as close as she could.

It had just stopped snowing, and the traffic had produced an abundance of slush in front of the Wal-Mart doors.

As I hobbled to her car, she got out of the driver's seat and came around to help me get in. Any doubt about whether or not this was the thing to do vanished.

She explained that she and her husband had a ministry in downtown Minneapolis. One of the young people who had come into their path many years before was coming to supper for his birthday, at their invitation, so if I didn't mind the commotion as she completed her meal preparations, I was most welcome.

We talked easily during the short ride to her home. She and her husband had raised six children, now grown. She helped me into the house and took my coat; there was a delicious smell of cooking venison. She tended to her dog and asked me if I minded preparing a pineapple upside-down cake. I immediately said I would love to help, even though I didn't have a clue as to how to make it. It felt so good to be able to do something, and I was actually in someone's home in a kitchen! She was so gracious, and left me to figure out this daunting task by handing me a cake mix, a cake pan, a can of pineapple rings, and the other items I needed.

I remember the rush of energy I felt as I actually got to work in the kitchen, and my delight in doing this small task took on great meaning. Today, whenever I prepare a cake mix, I thank God for the gift of the use of my limbs.

Suddenly, I wasn't tired. I was so glad to finally do something useful, even though I was weak and had to hold onto the kitchen counter as I mixed the batter.

After I finished the cake, my new friend prepared a chair and footstool for me and I settled in. Her husband arrived, and soon three young people in the living room were all chatting easily with this unassuming couple and me.

As I looked at the Christmas tree in the corner of the living room, I felt transported to a different place. More people wandered into the dining room while I was busy taking in the scene and I truly wondered if it was all a dream; maybe I was in the script of *It's A Wonderful Life*.

After we gathered around the table and prayed, we ate the most wonderful meal of my life. This woman, Laurie, a stranger I had known a mere three hours, had prepared this feast, and visited with me as if she had known me all her life.

In the living room after supper, three more young people arrived, slipped off their coats, and found places to sit on the floor. It now seemed ridiculous that I had questioned this woman's sincerity. I never wanted the evening to end, and for once, I didn't even think about my foot.

When we returned to the motel later that evening, she asked if she could pick me up for worship the next day. I now noticed that I had been on my feet longer than I had been for weeks. My right foot was throbbing, so I thanked her and told her I would call her. She thanked me for giving her the chance to get to know me!

The next morning my foot was no better, so I called quite early to thank her and then wrote her name and address in my address book.

She obviously is an angel, because after I returned home, I could not locate her name, number, or address in my address book where I had been doubly sure to write it down. I have looked endlessly and it simply isn't there, so I just tell the story of this miraculous day to others, and I thank God daily for it.

Nineteen
Looking and Listening

At the end of my third week of treatments, I developed terrible pain in my right ear. It became so severe that I couldn't make it through a treatment and had to ask to have the compression stopped. How I regretted that, because I knew it was an inconvenience for the other patients.

Out of the chamber, the doctor took a look and found fluid behind the eardrum. As a child, I'd had an infection of the mastoid bone in that ear and many ear infections from that time on. Now I would have to have a tube inserted through the drum to let the fluid drain.

The next day was Saturday. I couldn't tolerate the pain, so I decided to go to the emergency room.

The shuttle took me downtown and I registered at the ER and took a seat. The wait seemed long, although it was no more than an hour.

The physician told me I did have fluid behind my eardrum and it would be good to have a tube inserted so I could continue the hyperbaric treatments. He wrote me a prescription for something to ease the discomfort of the pressure I felt in my ear, and I hobbled the long distance to the pharmacy.

Many people were waiting to have their prescriptions filled, and I knew standing all that time was not an option. However, there was only one open seat. In spite of my exhaustion, I hesitated. A man heavy with silver chains and tattoos sat on one side of the open seat. I had never seen anyone with so many tattoos. The man on the other side looked like he needed a bath, and needed it yesterday. These people didn't look too savory. Would one of them try to take my purse?

To my surprise, both of them made room for my crutches as I maneuvered to sit down between them, and the young tattooed man immediately asked if I needed help. Helpful people just kept appearing, and I didn't get it!

I didn't bother to ask either of them how they were, just got my prescription and called the motel for a ride. It had been a very long afternoon, my ear hurt, and I wanted to get back to my room.

I waited in the glassed-in pick-up area at Hennepin General, an area I had been told not to wait in alone. What choice did I have? I was weak, on crutches, and without transportation. As I nervously waited for the familiar Days Inn shuttle, a young man, dark-skinned and tremendously tall, came into the pick-up area. He paced—almost ran—back and forth from window to window, crying and babbling.

This was my worst nightmare. He had to be the reason I had been told not to wait alone.

Out of the blue, he asked if I knew he was sixteen years old.

He didn't look at me, but I was the only other person there, so he must have been talking to me. I could hear distress in his voice and I said I was sorry; I couldn't tell his age.

He then said he was old enough to be told what was going on with his mother—why couldn't he know?

As he spoke faster and faster, I realized he had come from his mother's hospital room. He had been trying to talk to her but she wasn't responding. He didn't know what to do or where to go. Because he was a minor, no one would release any information to him.

He was so distressed that he paced like a scared baby rabbit. Sobbing and shaking, he met my gaze and took a step back, as if realizing for the first time that he had an audience. He brushed his arm across his eyes as if to wipe away any sign of weeping, raised both arms above his head, and approached me.

I looked up at him, so tired from standing I was hardly able to hold up myself up on my crutches. He stood—all 6'8" of him—just inches from me and asked if he could pray for me.

I raised my eyebrows in disbelief. I wanted to run. I shook my head, cleared my throat, and "No" came as a whisper from deep within me.

He laid very large hands on my shrinking shoulders anyway and said, "God, heal this child and take away her pain. Amen." His hands loosened their grip and slid off my shoulders. He walked away, mumbling something unintelligible, and disappeared into the night.

Following the sound of his words and direction of his voice, I looked toward the automatic doors, and there stood the Days Inn shuttle, shining white, fresh from the carwash, like a carriage awaiting me. I must have arrived in heaven! I got in and felt drenched by incredible warmth, though the temperature had dropped to -5 degrees.

As soon as I boarded the shuttle, I glanced again at the waiting area. For a few seconds, an aura surrounded it, so bright I could not look directly into the light. Was I imagining what had just taken place? I had never before felt such a sense of peace. This wasn't just a feeling; it was an intense shiver throughout my body that went straight to the core of my being faster than I could blink; it truly was a sense of being lovingly folded in someone's arms as though I knew the feel of God's hand reaching inside me, lifting me up and smiling at me. I felt weightless. Any burden I had ever carried was gone. Was this a vision of heaven, or a brief visit *to* heaven?

This experience moved me like none other before or since; I believe I actually did see the light of heaven, and I wake to it every morning still, just as I did that night. I glanced down and actually saw the light pass through me as though I were transparent. I saw it soar through the night sky like a comet and go on forever. This light shook me, made me limp; I had to hold myself steady in the shuttle or I would have dropped to my knees. It happened in such an instant that I momentarily forgot I had a cast on my leg.

The weight of that cast, and all the casts to come, never bothered me again. In fact, I walked on my crutches effortlessly for the next five months and never once complained about finding them inconvenient.

Today, every time I see a pair of crutches, I think of that night and feel lighter than air. I remember the final line from the poem "Footprints in the Sand": "It was then that I carried you." I never again noticed the marks the crutches made; from that time on, all I saw was one pair of footprints.

I pray for everyone I see using crutches that they may view them with the vision I was given, and may in turn share this miracle of a memory.

Twenty

Look Where You're Going

The tube was scheduled to be inserted Monday. This time, the shuttle dropped me off on the east side of Hennepin County Medical Center.

I was disoriented, because coming into the ER on Saturday, I'd gone in through the west doors. I kept asking for directions, but pretty soon I'd been walking a long time and felt lost. I sat down on a hallway bench and tried to get my bearings.

A young girl, maybe twelve years old, approached me and said "Hi" with a sweet smile. That was enough to buoy my spirits. I got up, determined to make it to the end of the hall. I walked through a hall that seemed to go on forever, then another fifty yards, then another right turn, and I was at the ENT registration desk for my 8:30 a.m. appointment.

Since I'd come into the ER on Saturday, I hadn't made it onto the weekly schedule and no one could find my name. The woman on duty picked up her appointment book and headed to another room.

I stood and waited until I couldn't stand anymore and had to sit down. I wondered, was I even at the right desk? I was so tired from walking all that way; I was sure I wouldn't find my way back, wherever "back" was.

But the lady returned, smiled, and told me, yes, I was in the right place.

What a relief! If there was no tube, there would be no hyperbaric treatment. No hyperbaric treatment, and . . . that was all the further I could think.

The tube insertion went smoothly, without pain. But now, how was I going to get to the hyperbaric chamber? If I hurried, I could get there in time for the day's second round, but I had never walked there from Hennepin County Medical Center alone. It wasn't far away—only two and a half blocks or so—but it was windy and snowing outside.

Anxiously, I asked four different people to point me in the direction of the chamber and I received four different sets of directions. I finally found an exit, stepped outside, and at once felt how cold it was. I didn't even know what direction I was facing. Nothing looked the way it had the day my husband and I toured the chamber. Time was getting short, and I started to panic.

I found a bench, sat down, and asked two women waiting for the bus if they knew where the chamber was. One said she knew of a coffee shop near the chamber. She called me "Honey," helped me up, and walked me to the intersection and then across the street. We walked for a block and found it!

I was so thankful I gave her a hug, dropped my crutch, dumped my purse, and nearly fell in a snow pile. She retrieved my crutch and the fallen money and asked if I could make it from there. If not, she'd wait for the next bus and take me farther.

I began to cry. I told her how grateful I was, but that I could make it myself from that point.

She said, "God bless you, honey," turned, and walked away, and I made it to the treatment on time.

Twenty-One
Look—There's Help!

*I*t was time to wash clothes.

I inquired at the front desk and learned the washers and dryers were on the seventh floor of the motel. My room was on the fifth. What was I to do? I didn't have a laundry bag and was in no shape to carry one. Wayne had remembered to pack Tide and dryer sheets, but how was I going to carry all this?

To my surprise, one of the women who worked in housekeeping offered to wash and dry my clothes.

I looked at her in disbelief. Who would offer to wash the clothes of a stranger?

Nonetheless, I accepted her help with gratitude. To this day, I don't know how I would have managed without her.

Twenty-Two
Looking at a New Cast

It was three weeks into my stay and I was scheduled to go to Mayo for a cast change. Three weeks was the schedule I'd been on for cast changes and that did not change; they continued to be scheduled although we hadn't discussed what would happen next. At each cast change, the incision was checked for healing. I knew this was important, but I had no idea how I was going to get from Minneapolis to Rochester, seventy-five miles away. The only ride I knew was the shuttle from the motel to the chamber.

Don, the shuttle driver, walked me through the process. I would board the shuttle from the hotel. He would drop me off at the Metrodome Light Rail stop. I would take the Light Rail to the airport, find the Rochester Direct Shuttle registration desk, board the shuttle, and be on my way to Rochester within a half hour. Nothing to it!

After Don dropped me off at the Light Rail, I crutched my way to the waiting area and searched my pocket for the dollar bills I needed for fare. Somewhere on the hike, I had lost my gloves and my hands were very cold. I fumbled around but couldn't find any money. I heaved a sigh. I was getting nervous; the Light Rail was due to arrive very soon.

A well-dressed older man walked by me but I ignored him, wondering what to do. He stopped and asked if he could help. I told him my dilemma and he inserted money into the machine and escorted me to the waiting area.

"Not a problem," he said when I thanked him, and took off in the direction from which he had come.

I boarded the Light Rail, got off at the airport, and had no idea where to go. What's more, there was no one to ask.

I walked toward the escalator. There was only one way to go—up. With the help of many, many people, I finally made it to the shuttle reservation desk. It was just ready to leave, and the driver helped me board. I wasn't looking forward to this trip, but I didn't think it could be worse than the one where they'd talked about amputating my foot, so I relaxed.

The ninety-minute trip went quickly. The shuttle stopped at the Kahler Hotel across the street from the Mayo Clinic and I headed out on my crutches. An attendant greeted me and helped me into a wheelchair and into Methodist Hospital. Once again in the cast room, I waited after my cast was removed, for what news, I really didn't know.

The surgeon came in, looked at it, and said it looked better.

I held on to that news—it looked better! I didn't really know what that meant, but I still had my foot.

The surgeon still talked about amputation, but he did say that "If it got better"—not that he knew it was getting better, or would get better, but if it *did* get better—I could think about having my foot reconstructed.

Whoa! "Reconstructed"? This was a new phrase, and I liked it.

The nurse returned to apply a new cast. We talked about all kinds of things. I laughed and giggled for the first time in a very long time. This was the second time I had the good fortune of having my cast removed by the same person. I noticed that the people around him enjoyed kidding him, which he clearly enjoyed. He was nicknamed "Shrek" and had a "Shrek" sticker over his name on his name tag. We talked about Christmas and presents, and I'll never forget what he told me. He said he and his wife had sons and the sons enjoyed hunting with him, making it a "guys only" activity, and they wanted to find a way to include his wife so she would feel a part of it. They had decided to get her camouflage pajamas for Christmas. He wanted to know what I thought of this, and I could tell he so wanted my approval.

I stifled a giggle, because I thought it both humorous and endearing. I told him that if it had been me, I would have appreciated their thoughtfulness. This desire to include his wife truly came from his heart, and I still find it precious because it was so important to him. I was nearing another complete cycle of using all the colors of casts, so he asked if I'd like a green and red cast for Christmas. That sounded colorful, so I agreed. When I was wheeled to the lobby, my brand new cast was red with green stripes, quite a sight.

Since I had about an hour and half before the shuttle would take me back to Minneapolis, I decided to have lunch at the cafeteria. I unlocked the wheels on the wheelchair and off I went. Hmm, a dilemma. How was I going to get through the line in a wheelchair holding a tray and picking out food?

A Mayo employee came along and immediately offered to take me through the line. The whole line was gracious and patient. I remembered I was in a clinic where this happened hundreds of time every day, but I was still grateful for the understanding. The food tasted so good, different from the usual microwave food I cooked for myself every day.

Time passed quickly while I visited with a couple from Iowa. I glanced at my watch. The attendant had assured me someone would check in and escort me to the van, but time was passing and no one came.

I became nervous. I wasn't very good at maneuvering a wheelchair. What to do? I tried to wheel my way up the ramp that led from the cafeteria in the subway level of the Gonda Building to the walkway but I backslid at least three times before a kind man pushed my wheelchair the rest of the way up. When he asked what he could do for me, I said I had less than twenty minutes to get to my ride. He went to the information desk and the woman there picked up her phone. Within minutes, an attendant appeared, double-checked the location I was looking for, and got me there on the double. I was so thankful. He seemed to have appeared from nowhere, like so many others within the last month.

When we arrived back in Minneapolis, I knew I would have trouble trying to backtrack from the airport. The shuttle driver offered to help me find my way back to the Light Rail and I thanked him; I knew he was tired but going out of his way to help me. And, most astounding and miraculous, when I boarded the Light Rail for the Metrodome station, standing there was the same man who had helped me that morning, paid my fare, and got me to the waiting area.

He nodded, smiled, and said, "Hello again; how can I help you this time?"

His smile showed that he saw my utter amazement.

I wasn't sure where to get off the Light Rail to catch the motel shuttle. He said he'd call the motel shuttle for me if I gave him the number.

I couldn't believe it! My fingers were still cold because I didn't have my gloves, but by the time I got off at the Metrodome, the motel shuttle was waiting for me.

I turned to thank the man for his kindness, and for the second time that day, he was gone.

Twenty-Three
Look at the Choices

*I*t was getting close to Christmas.

I wondered, how would I show my family I loved them and thanked them for their support, when I had no means to do so? I hadn't gotten any presents, nor could I get anywhere to buy any. I cried many times about the fact that I wouldn't be home for Christmas and that my husband couldn't take more than Christmas Day to see me because he'd already used up all his vacation time seeing to my care.

Even though Wayne never complained, I felt that any attempt to thank him just couldn't come close to everything he'd done to help me. Once, just once, when my foot hurt so terribly that I didn't know if I could keep on going, he had said, "You have to, because you want to be able to walk out in the backyard hand-in-hand with your grandchildren." Both my daughters were expecting babies, but I was preoccupied with getting my health back and I hadn't looked that far ahead.

I remembered the day we arrived at the hotel. Particularly, I recalled my husband's surprise at seeing the Little Dearborn Ford store across the street. He'd mentioned ordering parts there for his Model A many years before.

I knew how much his 1929 Model A meant to him. He'd bought it years ago when he graduated from high school and then restored it. He loved getting it running in the spring and riding in small town parades. I think what he loved most was the looks on people's faces when he honked the horn.

Here I am at Days Inn University, Christmas Day, 2007

I'd had good intentions about embroidering dishtowels, but I just didn't have the energy to do it, so I decided to hobble over to the Ford store to see if I could find something for Wayne. It was very cold, and just walking across the street was tiring because I was only used to walking to the shuttle and back, but I made it.

The man working there greeted me, then returned to his paperwork. I looked around for something that seemed like a Christmas present. I told the man my husband had a Model A and had ordered parts there years before. He pointed me toward some books on the history of Model A's and I was thankful—at least I would be able to give Wayne something he was interested in.

I made my purchase and decided to venture to the Greek deli and restaurant next door. I walked in and slowly took in the enticing aroma. It had been so long since I'd been in a restaurant!

In the deli, the dates looked delicious. The man behind the counter asked if I'd like to try one. Would I! I love dates and these were huge. He gave me another, and kept me supplied with dates my entire stay.

When Wayne came on December 24, I was so glad to see him. We decided to replenish my groceries, since I didn't know how many more treatments

I would need. By now, I'd had over twenty, and I had often heard people mention that twenty treatments was considered to be the first round. This important task complete, we went to a matinee and out to dinner at Perkins.

To have a simple meal together, to have this sweet, understanding man across the table from me—how many times had I taken for granted going out to eat with him? What a gift it is to be blessed with each other's company. He is truly my best friend, standing beside me at every turn.

As we ate, the manager came by with pies, asking a dollar apiece for them. They would be closed Christmas Day and the pies wouldn't keep, so we bought one.

As we left the restaurant, people were standing in line for pies. I remember one elderly woman leaning on a cart, and I wondered if it held all her earthly possessions because her grip on the handle was so tight. Her face looked wizened by the ravages of the cold and I had a urge to brush her hair; it was long and thick and I hoped it warmed her neck. She had a Perkins pie balanced on top of her cart and she offered me a piece. I had been able to order anything on the menu and had a very full stomach, yet she wanted to share what little she had with me.

My eyes welled up. What hit me hard was, "How can I, who have so much, appreciate it so little?"

My stomach churned. I wished I could have thought of something to offer her, instead of just "No thanks," and "I wish you a Merry Christmas."

I felt small. It was beginning to sink in just how much I truly did have.

Twenty-Four
Look at These!

As I returned to the HCHC for a treatment, I was glad to be back; I had missed the staff and other patients. Although it had only been three days since I'd been there, I had become used to being called if the chamber was opened for any emergencies and this was the longest I had gone without a treatment, as it had been closed Christmas Day.

When I walked in, the husband of one of the patients handed me a package, grinned, and told me to take a look.

Inside the bag, I found a red canvas bootie for my cast and two red bags, about six-by-ten inches long with Velcro handles, to hang from the top of my crutches.

One of the former patients had commented on how concerned she was about my bare toes sticking out of my cast every day, and she'd sewn a boot to cover my foot. She'd completed her treatment and was gone now, but had left these gifts as a surprise Christmas present for me.

I immediately tried the boot on and it fit. I likewise fastened the bags to each of my crutches and attached the Velcro handles. Hurrah! I would no longer have to carry a purse!

Gratitude overwhelmed me. How thoughtful and considerate! For months, my toes had gone uncovered, sticking out of the cast because it was too hard to keep a sock on. This lady hadn't been well when we'd first met, but she'd improved as the weeks went by.

I was glad she'd gotten to go home, but I was sorry I didn't know how to reach her to thank her. These items were so precious to me, more so because they were from someone I hardly knew who had performed this labor of love out of pure generosity, even though she herself was sick.

Twenty-Five
Look Who's Here!

December 13, 2007

My friend Pam is an angel, even more so because she doesn't know it.

Pam serves.

By contrast, I haven't always served willingly. In fact, I've always been somewhat hesitant to give of myself, my time, my talents, or possessions.

When Pam called, she asked a simple question. Would I like some company, probably after Christmas?

Pam, whom I had not seen for at least two years, was going to come 250 miles to celebrate a belated Christmas with me—me? Would I like that? How about if she brought her daughter?

Pam is such a dear person. She and her husband were Wayne's close friends for many years before he and I ever met, and the three of them shared many good times and bad. As I was getting to know Wayne, he told me about his involvement with weekend retreats at local churches in which Pam and her husband and family also participated that had created a very strong bond among them. Wayne had grown so much spiritually, and he wanted me to have the chance to experience a weekend retreat because through such retreats he and many of his friends and family had found "the peace that passeth all understanding."

Surprise visit! Renae Hanson, me, Pam Kronbeck, and Melissa Keith, December 28, 2007

I met Pam on my first retreat. Looking back, all I can think is, "Poor Wayne." He really had to talk to get me to go to a retreat. I liked being in control and knowing what I was getting into, and he just wouldn't reveal any details.

Meeting Pam in this environment created an incredibly powerful bond. In fact, she was the one who encouraged me to "jump off the diving board" and trust that Wayne was a good man. That bond has remained unbreakable and irreplaceable.

Pam's call left me speechless. I didn't know what to say, so I cried. I hadn't yet had any formal company at the Days Inn, but I was in the company of angels the whole time and didn't know it. Now someone was willing to come all that distance to see me and celebrate Christmas, stay overnight, and have some "girl time."

When Pam and her daughter Melissa came into Room 517, they gave me such warm, embracing, sustaining hugs. They didn't say anything, just looked toward the door to my room. I stopped and turned around.

Standing there, waiting to surprise me, was my friend Renae. I hadn't seen her for many years either. My heart overflowed and I cried. They told me to stop it but I just couldn't. These people had driven so far in such cold weather. This was a season for families, and I could hardly believe they had come to visit me.

Not only did they come, they'd brought hors d'oeuvres, and lots of them. It was too much, but I was overjoyed. I hadn't laughed, cried, or eaten so much in a very long time. We rented the movie *The Game Plan* and I've watched it many times since. It was an interesting choice of movies; it showed just how much we think we are in control when we really don't have a clue! I don't recall what time we went to sleep, but it didn't matter. I was among dear, dear friends.

The next day, we decided to visit a health food store. On my shuttle ride back from Rochester, I'd talked with a woman who knew a lot about health foods and I was sure there was another "cure" to be found there. We got quite lost, but my friend had a GPS, so we finally found the store. With no parking spot in sight, we decided it would be best for me to wait in the car while they went in.

I didn't care; just riding in a car and breathing fresh air in the company of dear friends was enough of a treat. My friends picked up the items the woman had recommended and I was so excited. Not only was I getting new life from oxygen, now I would be getting all that optimal nutrition as well.

When the time came, I hated to see my dear friends go, but I was thankful they had given the gift of their time and I was honored to be treated as family by them. Before they left, we prayed together, for a safe return, for peace and good health in our lives, for great fellowship, and for further healing of my foot.

It was another tough goodbye.

Twenty-Six
Looking at a Mistake

$\mathcal{I}$ was getting stronger. One day not long after Pam, Melissa, and Renae's visit, I decided to take the shuttle to the downtown Barnes & Noble. I had ridden past it many times, coming and going from the chamber, and I yearned to get my hands on some new reading material. Since I collect and restore dolls, I thought it would be fun to see what they had on that subject. I would be coming home to boxes of dolls that needed restoration, so I had a good reason to make the trip. I'd just find a sofa or a comfortable chair for a couple of hours; surely that wouldn't hurt my foot.

The shuttle driver asked how long I would be at Barnes & Noble. I thought an hour wasn't too long. In fact, at that moment, I was sure I could manage several hours. Impulsively, I decided I would stay from 2:00 until 5:00, crutch around the rows of books, and get some new reading material.

Imagine my surprise when I found this Barnes & Noble had no couches or chairs. Now what would I do? I couldn't sit on the floor because I wouldn't be able to get up, so I leaned against the bookshelves and tried not to think about the throbbing in my leg. It was a Saturday, and the shuttle was busy taking other guests around the city, so I decided the best thing to do was find a place to sit and wait.

I finally had to give up and sit on the floor, even though it was tough to get down.

Later, trying to get up was even more painful. As if it were timed, a kind woman asked me how she could help. She had clearly been shopping a while—her hands were full of bags and she looked weary. I tried to decline, but she would have none of that.

Between the two of us and the bookcase wall, I got back into a vertical position and she walked with me as I made my way to the elevator and back down to street level. She also offered to take me wherever I needed to go.

I hadn't thought I would meet any more angels in the city, but I was wrong. I thanked her and said I just needed to get to where the shuttle would stop.

She walked with me about a block and asked if I was sure I would be okay. I was sure. The shuttle would be here in about ten minutes, so I leaned against the wall of a restaurant.

By now, it was dark and I noticed police cars circling the block every ten minutes or so. Where was the shuttle? This was unusual. I was alone, downtown, with no gloves, carrying my wallet and identification in the red Velcro bag attached to my crutch. Every so often, I was greeted by people coming in and out of the restaurant.

One young man asked what had happened to me. I told him and he said, "God bless you," a phrase I was getting accustomed to hearing.

By this time, the shuttle was twenty minutes late and three police cars had gathered at a corner about a block and a half away. People were gathering too, and again I wondered what was going on. It was beginning to look a bit suspicious. Also, I was becoming very, very tired. I could no longer stand up, so I sat down against the brick wall of the restaurant.

A couple came out of the restaurant and asked if I was hungry and if they could buy me something to eat.

Their offer amazed me, and I said no.

They practically insisted, but I told them I was fine. I was so touched at the kindness of these strangers that I started to cry.

When I finally spotted the shuttle, I'd never been so happy to see a ride in all my life. That was the first and last time I ventured out on my own. I simply wasn't strong enough. If I had fallen, I can't imagine what would have happened, and I didn't really need to buy anything anyway.

Twenty-Seven
Looking at Another
Mayo Visit

January 6, 2008

This was the day I was due for a cast change at Mayo, and hopefully some news of what was in store for my leg. Again, I boarded the shuttle early in the morning and was dropped off at the Light Rail stop at the Metrodome. I deposited my money in the machine and got a ticket for the Light Rail, then realized I was waiting on the opposite side of where I needed to board. I had very little time in which to find a way over the railing to the opposite side of the track and there was nothing I could do except try to stride over it; if I fell, I fell.

I dug one crutch in the hard-packed snow, threw my good leg over the railing, and let myself fall into the snow bank.

I didn't fall too hard, but I'm not sure which I felt more—stupid or uncoordinated. Still, it was getting just a little easier to get around.

The walk around the airport was likewise less difficult, and I made it to the Rochester Shuttle. I had to ask for directions again several times, but this too was getting easier.

When the cast came off this time, I noticed something I hadn't seen in a very long time. Leg hair was actually growing on the ankle of my right foot! A strange thing to be excited about, but it meant something was circulating and working in that ankle.

When the doctor came to look at my leg, he said I was still looking at choices. One, of course, was amputation.

In a voice I can barely remember using, I asked if he would consider reconstructing my foot. To my great relief, he said yes! He talked about how it would be done and what materials he would use, from coral calcium to cadaver bone to ceramics to my own bone graft.

I don't recall much more of what he said, but I definitely remember what he said as he left the room: "I will do my very best for you."

I knew he meant every word.

Part Three
Looking Up

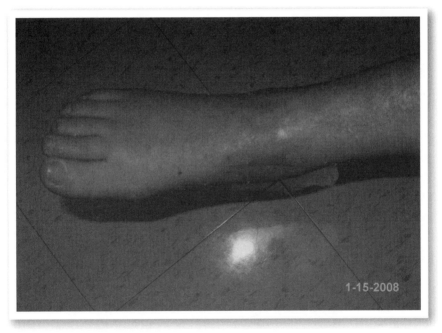

My right foot after twenty hyperbaric oxygen treatments, January 2008

Twenty-Eight
Looking at Waiting

January 14, 2008

Back home, this was the day my first granddaughter was scheduled to be born. I had returned home for the big event, but if I was going to get to see this new little person, she would have to be born before noon, because my reconstructive surgery was scheduled at Mayo the next day, January 15, and we had to make the six-hour trip yet today.

My daughter was induced at 7:00 a.m. and I stayed with her as long as I could, but it didn't look like the birth would happen before I had to leave. God had His own plan for the time this precious little one would come into the world.

Wayne came to the hospital just before 1:00 p.m. and said it was time to go, and I reluctantly left the room. My precious grandbaby would be born whether I was present or not.

In the bitter cold, we made the long drive to Rochester and checked into the motel. Neither of us knew what to expect the next day, so we passed the time in light-hearted conversation about Wayne's work and how we would certainly remember this unusual holiday season.

Just as we settled in to sleep, the phone rang. My precious granddaughter had been born at 11:14 p.m. that evening, a very healthy eight-pound baby girl.

What a wonderful gift to look forward to! My first grandchild would be waiting at home for me to hold!

The next morning, we checked in early at the hospital. I was eager and excited—this gifted surgeon was willing to undertake reconstruction on a foot once thought beyond repair. After all the prep work was done, I was off to surgery.

In the operating room, I received spinal anesthesia. Shortly after it took effect, the PA entered the room and lifted my leg.

I panicked, because even though it seemed to be attached, I couldn't feel it! She was wrapping it and I couldn't feel it! Did this bode well for what was to come?

Twenty-Nine
Looking at Good News

When I woke up, I still had my foot!

I said a prayer of thanks and started to sob. Two nurses were immediately at my side. I told them why I was crying and they both smiled.

This was what I'd been waiting for all these months, and it was worth everything I'd been through. I was still groggy and knew nothing else at the time, just that I had my foot, and that was enough.

I fell asleep and slept long into the evening. The surgeon stopped by later to tell me the six-hour surgery had gone well. He had been able to reconstruct my foot and was very pleased.

Months later, the PA from Infectious Diseases told me I was "Mayo's surprise."

Thirty
Looking Like Home

January 19, 2008

After my release from the hospital, four days post-op, though I longed to return to Minneapolis and continue the hyperbaric oxygen treatments for as long as it took, first I had to see my first grandchild. If I could just go home for a couple of days and see that baby, I knew I would be content to return to Minneapolis to complete my treatments. I was halfway through, and this would get me all the way.

Wayne lovingly settled me into the back seat for the trip home. It was exhausting and my leg throbbed, but all I could think of was seeing my precious granddaughter. Visions of her mingled with the doctor's final words to me: "Do not fall!"

When I got home, I tried hard to make it up the seven steps to the main level of our home. It exhausted me and I took three more steps until I just had to sit down. Then I glanced into the bedroom and could not believe my eyes. Lavender walls?

When I'd left, the walls were white. Was I seeing things? I took in the rest of the room.

There was a new headboard, a new bedspread, a new bed. The change surprised, even overwhelmed, me. Before, we'd had a soft-sided waterbed,

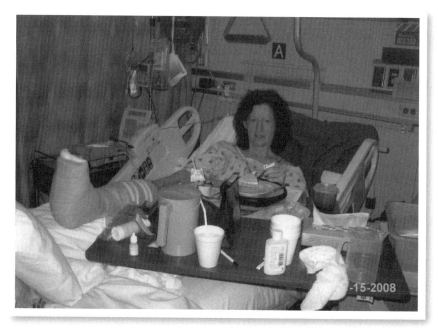

Here I am on January 18, 2008, ready to go home following reconstructive foot surgery

hard to get in and out of. We'd talked about getting a new bed, but Wayne had so much on his mind it never occurred to me he'd make it happen. Even the drapes were gone, replaced by a beautiful off-white valance trimmed in lavender, green, and gold. New horizontal blinds were also part of the makeover.

This was the bedroom I'd pictured long ago and hadn't thought about in a long time. Lately, my foot was the only thing on my mind—the first thing I thought of in the morning and the last thing I thought of before dropping off to sleep at night.

What a marvelous surprise! I would be able to easily get in and out of bed now; I probably wouldn't even need help. This was a wonderful gift, and a genuine labor of love.

Thirty-One
Looking for Strength

January 21, 2008

Wayne made a cold trip to my daughter's home and brought precious little Jayah to our house.

What a delight to meet and hold my granddaughter! I couldn't get enough of her. I thought she was the most beautiful baby I had ever seen.

The next morning, Wayne reluctantly returned to work and a nurse from Clay County came over to talk about the services I would need. She and the rehab specialist pored over the discharge summary and concluded I would need a lot of assistance. The two of them stayed several hours and discussed all my options.

I was very weak, and the doctor's remark, "Whatever you do, don't fall," rang in my ears. I thought that, now that my foot had been reconstructed, I would regain my strength fast. What I had forgotten was that I was used to living in a motel room the size of an efficiency apartment and wasn't used to doing much for myself. I wasn't even preparing meals for myself, other than the microwave kind. Still, I was determined.

When the nurse and rehab specialist left, I walked toward the stairway, not intending to go down, but then I tripped on my very large cast. I slipped all the way down the seven stairs and landed squarely on my right foot.

I cried. No, I sobbed. I knew no one would hear me, and I just had to let it out. The very last thing I had been told not to do, I had done.

I looked at my foot as though I could see whether something had moved out of place, but I couldn't tell.

What would I do now? It would do no good to call my doctor, six hours away, so I rolled onto my stomach and swung around. I was sweating so much I had to stop and assess what it was I was trying to accomplish. All I could think of was trying to crawl up the stairs, but this seemed monumental. Even if I could call 911, what difference would it make? I would be put in an ambulance, taken to the hospital, have an X-ray, and then find out if all the days and months I had just been through would have to be repeated.

Somehow, I crawled up the steps to the kitchen floor, lifted myself up just enough to reach the phone, and called 911. At that moment, it occurred to me that many angels were out there still, and I stopped crying. Calmly, I related what had happened and said I needed an ambulance right away.

In mere minutes, two people let themselves in as I had asked, came upstairs, put me on a gurney, and took me to the hospital. The doctor said X-rays would be taken right away. I lay quietly, praying for acceptance, and took deep breaths.

Months earlier, I had bought Faith Hill's CD *Breathe*, and now I remembered to do just that. God had brought me safe this far, and I truly believed He wasn't going to let go now. I wasn't in any extra pain, other than the usual post-surgical discomfort; I was just anxious. I kept telling myself, "What will be, will be." I also remembered how often I've thought that it's when we give up control that we have the most control, and I held onto this notion for dear life.

When the doctor returned with my X-rays, he said they would be sent electronically to Mayo, but it didn't appear that anything was damaged.

The relief that flooded me might have been premature, but it was still relief. What a blessing if nothing had been hurt!

Wayne came to the ER and took me home, and that night we talked about my care. Was there someone who could come in to be with me during the day? It was now clear I was in no shape to return to Minneapolis for hyperbaric treatments if I couldn't even walk thirty feet without falling.

But what was wrong with me? I had been so strong before the reconstructive surgery. How had I gone from being able to walk at least one-half a block in Minneapolis, getting around day to day by shuttle, making it to the shower, albeit somewhat awkwardly, to this? Granted, I'd worn out the knees of a pair of jeans and sweatpants both by crawling and sliding my leg from the bed to the bathroom of the motel each morning before I boarded the shuttle, but at least I'd been able to get around.

Quite simply, after fourteen surgical procedures, my leg was saying "enough already." It needed a rest.

The next day, the same health assessment folks came back to talk about my home care. The subject changed to rehabilitation, and we decided home was not the best place for that. I ached to be at home, but it just wasn't feasible. ManorCare Healthcare in Fargo had an opening, and meanwhile, the rehab specialist and nurse could look in on me.

Wayne called his mother. Could she help with meals for a couple of days? Bless her heart, she could.

For my part, "a nursing home" was all I could think of. I was only fifty-five and otherwise very healthy, but "otherwise" wasn't enough.

It was actually a rehabilitation center we were considering, but the words "nursing home" stung in my brain. I was not ready to accept this, but my choices were taken away. My fate was in everyone else's hands. I didn't like any of it, but I had no choice.

That night, I didn't sleep at all in the beautiful new bed my husband had so lovingly bought, and I wept for him. He would again have to look after me. This very loving stoic man had come down with shingles before I went to Mayo in 2007. He was fighting a tremendous battle of his own, and any words of comfort from me seemed hollow. I feared they would contribute more to the problem—me—than soothe. He had to be so tired.

The arrangements were made, and I packed even fewer clothes than I had for Minneapolis. Stubborn and determined, I decided that was somehow going to make my rehab stay shorter. I was to check in at 1:00 p.m. in two days. Meanwhile, a tooth that had abscessed had to have surgery in the near future or I wouldn't be entering the hyperbaric chamber at all, ever again.

The morning of my check-in at rehab, I went to the endodontist. At least I could get that tooth out of the way. I received the Novocain and waited until it took effect. The endodontist came in and started on the tooth, then stopped. He couldn't do the procedure because of a vertical crack in the tooth. It would have to be pulled. There was nothing else he could do.

I couldn't believe it! When I walked back into the lobby, Wayne looked at me in surprise. I told him what happened and we headed off to the rehab center.

When we arrived, I stepped out of the car, thinking, "This is a dream," but it wasn't. I was really here, standing outside our car at the nursing care facility.

Wayne grabbed my arm to help me across the icy parking lot and in we went. I was escorted to a bed and learned I had a roommate. She was a dear, this ninety-six-year-old woman. She had a wonderful daughter who came at noon every day to help her mother with her dinner. I asked her why she came every day, and she said her mother had taken such good care of her that this was a small thing to do to repay that.

Thirty-Two
Looking at Rehab

$\mathcal{M}$y stay at ManorCare was three weeks long and very humbling. My mother had spent the last three years of her life in assisted living in Fargo, and I didn't like the reminders being here gave me. I kept telling myself I was here for rehabilitation, not long-term care, and even though I wasn't the youngest person, I was far from the oldest.

I didn't quite know how to view the experience. The most beautiful memory I have of my stay at ManorCare was the time my daughter brought Jayah to my room. She was now three weeks old and a little angel.

My roommate looked at her, teared up, and held her arms out in position, ready to hold a baby. I saw the look in her eyes, this grand lady of ninety-six years, as she gazed at my granddaughter. The connection of their lives to each other was visible.

The rehabilitation care I received was superb. The loving, caring people who do this work have their hearts and souls in it; it's not just a job. It was hard to accept this stay as anything other than being in a nursing home, but I know it would have been impossible to recover without this tender loving care. I think of these individuals as angels of mercy, everyone from the administrators to the person who mopped the floors to the cooks and the activity director, who just happened to be from my hometown of Monango.

It was a delight and surprise to see this old acquaintance again. We'd formed a friendship in high school and belonged to the same church. Our paths hadn't crossed often in the thirty years since, but I'd always enjoyed her company and remembered with gratitude her visits with my mom whenever she did return to Monango for a visit.

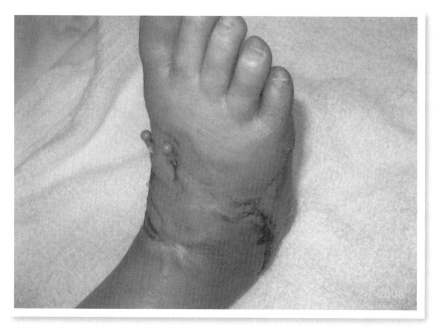

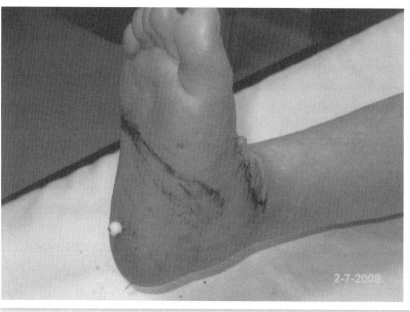

View of right foot after first cast removal February 7, 2008

Thirty-Three
Looking to Return

My twice-a-day-rehab workout at ManorCare was grueling and I was shocked at how weak I'd become. I'd always associated being trim with being in shape—big mistake. I couldn't even make it to the restroom on my own.

After three weeks, I was ready to go back to Minneapolis for more hyperbaric treatments. There was still the question of the tooth that could not be operated on because of the vertical crack, and I knew it would have to be extracted before I went back for more treatments. Wayne had to work, and I mentioned this to Pam when she came to visit me at ManorCare. Angel Pam, who also visited me in Minneapolis, said without a moment's hesitation that she was going to take me back to Minneapolis, and she refused to take no for an answer.

I tried to pay her for gas and food, and the note pictured below (see page 98) says it all. I still tear up to read that note. "It was my pleasure to serve you." How could she write that and mean it? That was true servanthood, but where was my sense of servanthood? Had I been selfish all this time? I prayed for less sense of self and more sense of others.

Pam stayed overnight and helped supply my room with necessities. We didn't know how long I'd be staying this time, only that I had an appointment at Mayo in several weeks and Wayne would drive to Minneapolis and take me to Rochester. That way, we could both visit with the doctor and find out my progress, if any.

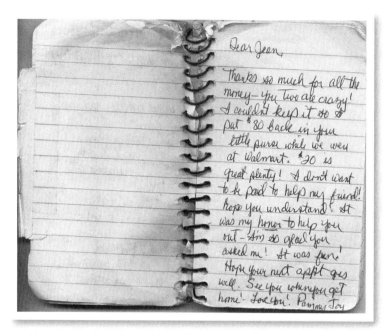

Pam's note to me about how thankful she was to be able to serve me, February 2008

It was hard to see Pam go. How could I ever repay her, even if she didn't think I needed to? Maybe someday I would be able to return the favor to her, or pay it forward. For now, I pray for her every day. There is no one like her.

While I was staying at ManorCare, the cat we'd had for eighteen years began to have major health problems. All the time I was away from home, Pookie had been company for Wayne, and he really loved that cat.

He called one morning shortly after I returned from a treatment to tell me the cat had died early that day. He was clearly in need of comfort, and my heart went out to him. I didn't know what to do except to say how sorry I was. When we hung up, I called Wayne's mother and asked if she could visit with him. He's a very private person, but I knew he needed someone to talk to.

By now it was March, and Wayne made plans to pick me up and take me to Rochester for the monthly checkup. Maybe this time we'd find out if there was any growth, any sign the reconstructive surgery had worked. We packed up my things about mid-afternoon so we could stay overnight in Rochester before my early morning appointment with the surgeon the next day. After a discussion with Dr. Collier at the HCHC, I learned I had come along very well and had completed the second round of treatments. He was actually releasing me from additional hyperbaric treatments!

It was very, very difficult to leave the comfort of the Days Inn, even though I longed to be home once more. I hesitated to think about the term "for good" because I no longer knew what that meant.

I had become so close to all these people. They had always anticipated my needs, treated me with respect, and given me hugs. The young people had become like my children, ones I would be proud to have, and the goodbyes were tearful. Thanks to this experience, I no longer say goodbye, I just say, "Until we meet again."

Several days earlier, I had taken the shuttle to a grocery store so I could buy a birthday cake for Don, the shuttle driver for nearly all my trips to the chamber. I surprised him with the cake and I'll never forget the smile on his face. Such a small thing for such faithful service.

Once in the car, Wayne and I chattered, our moods considerably lighter. The constant tension of the past several years had begun to fade just a bit, and I thanked God for this man at my side.

On the ride to Mayo, I got a call from my daughter who lived in Rochester. She and her husband were also expecting a baby girl, my second grandchild, and I was as eager for her arrival as for my first granddaughter. We'd made tentative plans to have dinner with them, but on the phone she said she didn't think she'd be able to make dinner. "You know, we're expecting a baby," she said.

"Of course I know!" I replied.

"No," she said, "we really are expecting a baby—I'm already in the hospital!"

She was in the early stages of labor and said she'd keep us posted. I knew I wouldn't be able to be at the hospital that night and it didn't look like the baby was coming very soon, so we made an early night of it. Unfortunately, I didn't sleep at all; I just waited for the phone to ring.

When we got up the next morning, there was still no news. My daughter was at the hospital next to the clinic where my appointment was held, so we planned on going there as soon as my appointment ended. Just before it began, we found out we had our new baby granddaughter, which made the morning so much more joyous.

We received more good news at the appointment. There were signs of growth in the foot! The surgeon looked at the x-ray very carefully for what seemed like an hour, then turned, looked me in the eye, and said healing was taking place.

I was on the examination table and my husband was sitting in a chair beside me. I will never, ever forget what happened next.

As soon as the surgeon spoke these words, Wayne's shoulders slumped and he began to sob. He wept for so long that I began to understand the toll this had taken on him. What a dear man. The look in his eyes as he lifted his gaze to me revealed pure joy and made chills come over me from the top of my head to the bottom of my toes. This was the day the Lord had made, and we were rejoicing and being glad in it!

I got another new cast, and another appointment in a month. If the signs of growth continued, perhaps the rods sticking out of the top and bottom of my foot could be removed and I could get a boot. A CAM walker at this point would be marvelous!

Thrilled with the news, we headed for the hospital to see brand new Kylie, and what a beauty! I of course thought she looked just like her grandma. Wayne took lots and lots of pictures, and then it was time for us to return home.

How blessed I was. Two granddaughters in less than four months, and my foot was healing. My cup indeed runneth over!

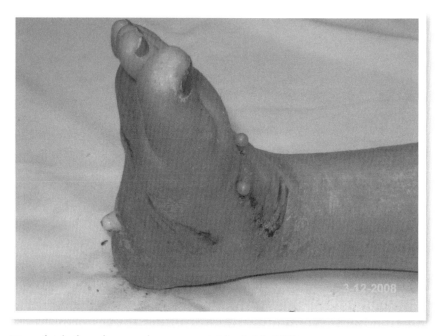

View of right foot after second cast removal, March 12, 2008

Thirty-Four
Looking from Home

When I returned home from Minneapolis in March, I walked into my closet and gasped out loud as I looked at the expanse of clothing in my five-foot closet. It looked like a women's department store, and I began to cry. What could I possibly do with all that clothing? It was too much; the clothes were just collecting dust.

I felt disgust run through me, and I methodically began to remove the pieces, folding them carefully, hobbling out to the bed on my crutches, and placing them into piles. With the bed half-piled with blouses and pants, I asked myself how I could have so much. These items belonged to and on someone else. When had I become a clothes collector? This closet was bigger than the space some people had in their entire homes. The thought embarrassed and disgusted me at the same time.

I decided then and there that all of them were going to be donated; I would keep only what I knew I would wear. I filled six large garbage bags and my closet was not yet empty.

Clothes, I admitted to myself, had become about the look, the cut, and the material, not about need. I felt ashamed and sad; I hadn't even noticed it happening.

To this day, I replace items only with what I know I will wear, and I feel blessed that I have choices.

Thirty-Five
Looking Straight Ahead

April 2008

I was healing, and my next appointment at Mayo was set for mid-May. Being home this time was much, much easier. Rehab had been effective, and I could get around on my crutches pretty well.

We had just finished a sunroom on the west side of the house, and when I got up each morning, I spent nearly the entire day resting there and taking in the sight of our backyard. I actually saw the buds of the leaves form. I don't think I've paid so much attention to the miracle of spring since I was a little girl. When the weather warmed early, I started to venture outside.

At my next appointment, the hardware that had been sticking out of my foot was removed. I graduated to a boot, and after that, I ventured outside each day to get the mail. Still, it took a few weeks for me to give up the safety of using my crutches. I hadn't realized how dependent I had become on them, how much I used them to steady my steps.

Gradually, very gradually, I gave them up as I began to put light pressure on my foot. The doctors had advised me to wait until June to drive, until I had returned to wearing a shoe, and I was glad to do so. What was the hurry now? I had gone this long without driving; certainly I could wait a few more weeks.

My dear friend Pam had promised long ago that when I was able to walk without crutches, she would take me shopping or out to eat, just so I could get out of the house. Truth is, Pam and I joked about turning fifty-five years old and how our figures had begun to "sag." We laughed and joked many times about going to Victoria's Secret to explore their "being 29 again" section—as though there was such a section!—and reminisce.

I just wanted to appreciate the ordinariness of watching other people. It was going to be so much fun to walk without always being mindful of watching out for that ankle and where to step. Although I had no desire to catch up on the "latest styles," I wanted to observe people and meet their glances with a smile, rather than have them watch me for a change. I knew that shopping would be very tiring and it was likely a great deal of trouble for Pam to take me out, but I was thankful. It had been so long since I'd been able to go out for anything but a medical appointment.

By May, I could not yet drive, but I was no longer using crutches, so I gave her a call. How good it would be to have a snack in a restaurant rather than heat up microwave food!

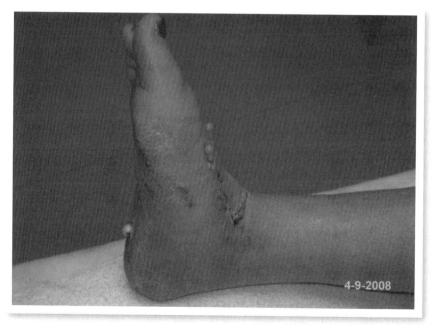

4-9-2008

View of right foot after third cast removal, April 9, 2008

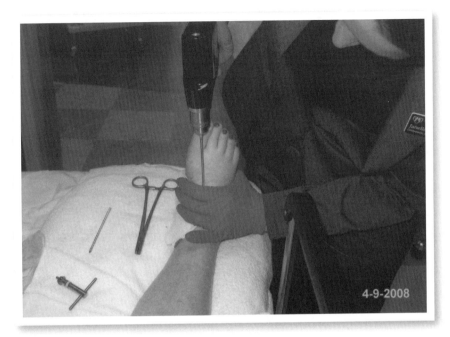

Removal of rods April 9, 2008

Thirty-Six
Looking at Relearning to Walk

There was now quite a bit of difference in the length of my legs, and I started physical therapy at ProRehab to relearn how to walk while putting weight on my right foot. Initially, I was in therapy three days a week for two and a half months followed by two times a week for four months. After that, I tapered off to one time per week for several additional months.

Tom, the therapist, was patient and pleasant. He joked with me and I looked forward to my therapy appointments, even though it was hard work learning to walk with a normal gait.

It also took months to figure out how to make an orthotic corrective piece for my shoes and how to build the sole. In November of 2009, I found that the most comfortable footwear was Birkenstock sandals, and Tom at Anderson Shoe Repair in Moorhead made the sole so expertly that I barely realized I had a foot that had given me so much trouble.

Now, even though I couldn't work full time, I could stand on the foot. I felt a little discomfort, but nothing compared to what I'd felt in the past.

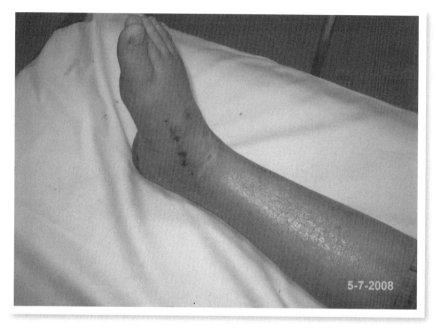

View of right foot after fourth cast removal May 7, 2008

Thirty-Seven
Looking toward Heaven

When I arrived in Minneapolis that first November and settled in for my several-months' stay, the movie *The Bucket List* was on my mind. I decided then and there to make a "bucket list" of my own. I knew I would never wear "regular" shoes again, because one foot was two sizes smaller than the other and my legs were different lengths, but at the top of my personal bucket list was walking again without crutches, boot, or cane.

I also very much wanted to sing with the Fargo-Moorhead Master Chorale, a group of dedicated musicians who love singing choral music. I love to sing, and I grew up singing in church, in school, and in college. It enriches my life, so in September of 2008, I decided to look up the chorale director, Lowell Larson, and find out how I might join the group.

I left a message, but days later I still hadn't heard from him. I thought maybe that meant I didn't have a chance of joining.

Several weeks later, Larson called and invited me to audition. I wanted to sing, but "nervous" doesn't begin to describe how I felt at the audition, held in the sanctuary of Trinity Lutheran Church in Moorhead.

Lowell sat down at the piano, told me to relax, and played a few notes to let me warm up. I tried to sing, but I was so nervous I was afraid I was going to start crying. I could barely get out a sound.

He then asked if I was a soprano. I said yes, and he played a series of notes and asked me to sing them. As I cleared my throat, I looked up and saw a magnificent stained glass window with a beautiful figure of Jesus high above the pipe organ in the balcony. His arms were outstretched and the words "Come Unto Me" were etched in the glass.

I could hardly believe my eyes. I took a deep breath and the notes came out, clear and relaxed, as I kept my gaze on His face. I felt so thankful, grateful, and humbled. I closed my eyes and immediately cried huge tears in amazement of the nearness of His presence.

Lowell told me I had a nice voice and was in the group and then I really cried. I felt truly blessed. Now, not only could I thank Him in words, I would be able to sing His praises in a group.

Thirty-Eight
Look Out!

December 10, 2008

The Master Chorale had been practicing that night, like nearly every night for weeks, preparing for four days of concerts. My daughter called and asked if I could watch Jayah for the evening while she spent some time with a friend who had been in a car accident.

Jayah always slept well at our house, dropping into a deep sleep whenever she visited. Surely she would fall into the same restful sleep she had so often before, but God had other plans.

Jayah was restless and still awake at 3:00 a.m. I hesitated to call my daughter, but no matter what I tried to do, Jayah was not going to be comforted. She wanted her mama and that was that. I lovingly put her in the car seat in the back of my car and we headed off to my daughter's.

Soon, I realized Jayah wasn't even stirring. I briefly considered turning around and heading back home, but I didn't think it would matter at this point—her mother was whom she wanted.

We got to my daughter's about 4:00 a.m. I knew my daughter had to work the next day, so she and Jayah went back to bed and I got back in my car and started for home.

Unbeknownst to me, when it had snowed lightly the day before, patches of black ice had formed on the road.

I began to swerve on Highway 10. I put my foot on the brake and heard a very loud screech. I steered in the direction my car was swerving and tried to stay on the right shoulder because of the car in the lane ahead of me. I swerved onto the right shoulder and thought I was clear to make the ditch, but instead I hit a utility pole nearly head-on.

Bam! I heard a sound like the popping of a BB gun. It was the air bags going off.

I looked at my right arm, but it was hard to move. The air bag had hit me with such force, I was afraid I'd broken something.

Glancing toward the dash, now hidden by the air bags, I remembered seeing the Perkins restaurant sign and having the impulse to go in for coffee.

As adrenalin kicked in, I pulled out my cell phone and punched in 911. I remember trying to report my location: "Well, I'm in front of Perkins on Highway 10. I don't see any street signs."

I was trying to think, but my right arm was throbbing. I looked at my fingers. They weren't broken. Good! I could still play the piano tomorrow and practice the songs for the Master Chorale concert that same night. After all, it was only 4:30 a.m. and the concert wasn't until 6:30 the next evening. Plenty of time for any swelling to go down.

Thirty-Nine
I Don't Like the Looks of This

The ambulance arrived along with a police car and someone asked if I wanted to go to the emergency room. I said yes, because I was afraid my right arm was injured. I did notice the slight look of disbelief the police officer gave me when I told him where I was going and why. How many fifty-six-year-old grandmothers are returning their grandchildren at 4:30 in the morning?

I was examined in the emergency room. Nothing was broken, thank goodness, but I was shaken, and I thanked God my granddaughter wasn't in the car. The thought of that baby in a car accident I had caused was more than I could bear.

I am ordinarily soft-spoken, and when I'm shaken, I tend to talk faster than normal. I didn't yet have the correct lift on my shoe, so I was also walking slower than usual, dragging my right foot.

All this raised the officers' suspicions, and they decided to administer a breathalyzer test at the hospital.

I was shocked, because I don't drink alcohol, any alcohol.

The officer administered the test twice, but nothing registered.

Two more officers arrived. One of them administered a test in which I had to look into a light. They noticed my right eye tended to move toward the center when it followed the light and I was disgusted. Of course it did! I have a lazy right eye. I've also had a vitrectomy performed on my left eye, along with the removal of a cataract.

113

Looking back now, I can see why all these things together would cause them to think there was something amiss, but I couldn't understand why I couldn't just leave.

Since my right foot is fused in three places, I couldn't perform the field sobriety test. However, I could place my right and left index fingers on my nose.

One of the officers asked if I would give a blood or urine sample. I said that was fine.

About this time, my doctor of twenty years appeared in the hospital hallway. I was so glad to see him! He asked what on earth I was doing here and I threw up my hands, because I didn't know either. He looked at the officers and shook his head in disbelief.

At that point, an officer came up and said he was going to cite me with a fourth-degree medical DUI charge, which I had never heard of. He told me I could go and that I had an initial court appearance in early January, 2009.

I didn't give all this much thought until the end of December, but as the date crept closer, I decided I needed an attorney, so I called the Vogel Law Firm in Fargo. Within minutes, Ken Kohler, an attorney with the firm, called me.

After I told him what happened, he said that in Minnesota, everything depended on the toxicology report. When that came back, we could do the paperwork to get the charge dismissed.

Forty
Looking Guilty?

January 13, 2009

For my initial court appearance, I met Ken at the courthouse in Moorhead. The day before, my doctor had written a note about my prescription medications. Likewise, my doctor from Mayo had sent a letter explaining the condition of my foot and the reason for my limp.

These letters explained everything, I thought. I didn't think about the fact that nothing could be decided until the report came back from the state toxicology lab, which ended up taking five months.

In the courtroom, my case was introduced. The judge said that prior to being able to hear my case, I would have to taken to the jail and booked.

Booked? Me? Was I under arrest?

All I could think of was how utterly stupid this was. I had worn a black-and-white striped scarf to court this dreary cold January day because it reminded me of Dr. Seuss' "The Cat in the Hat" and how silly some situations could be, and this was one of them. What was I doing in Clay County District Court, and why was I summarily sent away to be booked before I could make an appearance when I was already in court? How ridiculous.

Nonetheless, I heard Ken say, "Yes, your Honor," and we were off to the jail. My big, fat pride deflated like a balloon.

At the jail, everyone was busy. Ken politely asked how long it would be until I was booked and was told it would take about ten minutes. He needed to go back to court because he had other clients waiting; would I be okay waiting here by myself?

I knew I couldn't stand very long, but ten minutes didn't seem like forever, so I told him I'd be okay. It was twenty-one degrees below zero that morning and the waiting area wasn't heated.

After about twenty minutes, I could no longer stand up, so I sat down on the floor.

After I quit feeling sorry for myself, I prayed for understanding of the message that was being put in front of me. I didn't know what it was, but I was certain there was one somewhere in this experience.

Was I supposed to realize I should never judge others by their appearance? Did I think less of people who were in the same shoes I was now in? Did I need to be humbled in order to understand that I, too, was in need of God's grace?

I didn't know, but I didn't like being here, and I still thought it was absurd.

After nearly an hour, Ken returned and asked if anyone had helped me. I shook my head and he found me a stool where people sit when they visit folks in jail. The seat mattered more than the environment, and I welcomed the relief and the chance to get off the floor.

We waited some more and then walked into the area where fingerprints and mug shots were taken. By now it was nearly 11:00 a.m. My appearance had been set for 9:00, and I had a dental appointment at 11:00. I wondered what I was going to do. I needed to call my dentist, but I hadn't been allowed to take my cell phone into the courthouse. Besides, what was I going to say? That I couldn't make my appointment because I was being booked?

I told Ken my problem and someone found a telephone for me.

The receptionist at the dental office was concerned when I cancelled my appointment and wanted to know if I was feeling well.

What could I say? I said, no, I wasn't okay, but I'd explain later, and I apologized for the change in plans.

The finger printer never did get all ten of my prints taken and finally gave up. He was quite frustrated, mostly with himself; he said he'd been doing this for over twelve years and had never had had such a problem. He was thinking aloud, and he commented on the fact that women's fingertips tended to be harder to print because we do fine work, such as sewing, and besides that, the winter tended to dry out the skin to the extent that the prints were nearly indelible.

We were given permission to leave the detention center and return to the courtroom. By this time, I could no longer stand at all.

Ken quickly got a wheelchair, pushed me into the middle of the room, and spoke on my behalf. For a moment, I thought about what a sight I must have been. What a drama queen I must have appeared to be! Ken asked the Court for permission to contest the omnibus hearing; and to file a motion for a request to dismiss the charges.

The judge granted his request and we left, but I continued to get notices for court appearances because the toxicology report hadn't come back.

Finally, on April 14, the report came back. There were no painkillers, no sleeping medications, no controlled substances as defined by the state of Minnesota in my system; nothing that was not prescribed and nothing beyond its prescription was present. The state's attorney reduced the charge to "Duty to Drive with Due Care," a petty misdemeanor carrying a $40.00 fine. After all, I had hit a city utility pole and repairing it was quite costly to the city of Moorhead.

I signed the paperwork for the reduction in charge on my birthday, April 23, and treated myself to a patty melt, French fries, and a chocolate malt.

I was looking so forward to the evening. Wayne was taking me out for a wonderful dinner at a restaurant that had become a favorite of ours and carried many pleasant memories for us as well as having a reputation for delicious food and generous portions, but the restaurant I immediately went to was located just next to the law firm.

I hadn't treated myself to such "comfort food" in a long time. I was so relieved by what had just taken place that I wanted food that was just plain bad for me—the more calories, the better!

The next day, I received a notice in the mail stating my Minnesota driver's license was going to be revoked effective May 4, 2009.

I called Ken and he immediately got busy. He asked the court to waive the hearing and sent a letter to the state attorney general explaining the circumstances of the case.

After the fact, he told me rarely, if ever, does the Attorney General consider dismissing charges, but in my case ordered an immediate administrative rescission of implied consent revocation for the Court Administrator to strike from its calendar.

All I can say is, Ken Kohler, you rock!

Forty-One
Looking at Things
in a New Light

January 2009

After my next appointment with the orthopedic surgeon at the Mayo Clinic, one of the things I was determined to do was walk the clinic stairway without holding onto the railing or using crutches.

The clinic stairway is a beautiful staircase leading from the subway level of the Gonda Building to the first floor. I had never walked it without holding onto the banister, because my first trek on the staircase was in 2005 when I had a vitrectomy on my left eye and could hardly see. After that, I crutched it and grabbed the banister for support.

It's the simple things that matter, and I did it. Pam even took my picture on the stairway.

It was also a huge treat to be able to drive again. My foot has no "bend" in it, so I became comfortable driving with my heel. Now the car I have has an accelerator and brake that move back and forth.

Perhaps most important of all to me is having the ability to walk down the steps in the front of the house and onto the lawn. Walking on uneven ground was one of the last goals I had to meet before I graduated from physical therapy. Now I can walk thirty paces to the flower garden, sit on the ground, and watch the earthworms at work. I stare in wonder at the miracles of the growth of flowers and weeds, each identical to its kind and perfectly shaped, again and again and again.

All along, this was occurring while I was going about what I thought was important. Strange, because now my foot seems so insignificant compared to the miracle of nature and the wonder of God's creation around me.

Where was I while all this was going on? Where had I been all this time I had been blessed to be a miracle of His?

I have been broken and spilled out, and very lovingly and sparingly put together again only because of God's grace. I can think of no greater gift.

It took a transformation of my entire being, the giving up of my will to understanding and rejoicing in the fact that His will is being done and His unconditional omnipresent love and grace are with me always. The wonder of it all is that the best is yet to come.

Here I am walking up the stairs of the Gonda Building at the Mayo Medical Center—no crutches, no cast, no hanging on to the handrails, January 2009

Epilogue
Looking at Paying It Forward

When I originally set out to write this book, the overwhelming message I wished to convey concerned the healing power of oxygen. I now understand my story is about restoring health to my soul as well.

Two years have passed since I heard the news that was "bad, bad, very bad." Life now is "good, very, very good."

While I was in Minneapolis, I was the recipient of some of the kindest gestures possible. Complete strangers offered to help me. People in checkout lines told me they would think about me or pray for me.

I have had the rich experience of being broken and spilled out. I cannot think why God didn't give up on me, but His plan doesn't need to make sense to me; I only need believe in it. Because I cannot do so by myself, I pray for His mercy every day to continue to be raised up. When we are at the bottom, there is only one way to look, and that is up.

While I was in Minneapolis and alone in my hotel room, I had plenty of time to look up and reflect. What had I done with my life? Had I spent it on my own agenda, or had I appreciated each day as an opportunity to live in the light and be a light?

This self-analysis was not satisfying. I had forgotten that my life is intended for a higher purpose. That purpose includes embracing each day as it is, not as I wish it to be. Rather than being unhappy that it's too windy, too cold, too humid, too dry, too wet or "too" something, I need to remember that I am not in charge of the day. God has made each day according to His purpose, and I am to rejoice and be glad in it.

Today, my purpose includes offering thanks each morning for the life I have, the fact that I have my foot, and that I can walk.

Every day, I thank God that He chose to heal me.

Every day, I pray for all people, because we're all in this together.

Every day, I vow to tell everyone I love that I love them, every chance I get.

Every day, I thank people for their help whenever and wherever it's given, and return it or pay it forward as soon as possible.

Every day, I do my best to think positively. I have a new foot, a new attitude, another chance at life. I can think "up," look up, and be up. It is so much more satisfying than being negative. It is also easier to live with myself when I think of how much I have been given and therefore how much I have to give.

Every day, I engage in life.

Every day, I forgive others even as I wish to be forgiven. When I finally realized my infections were life-threatening, I became aware of how fleeting life is. The time we have to spend in harmony with one another is very short. I resolved to try to make peace with people I have hurt and ask their forgiveness. As a result, I do not let problems fester, nor do I bear grudges. I do not want unfinished business to get in the way of using the time I have with the people I care about.

Every day, I do my best to surround myself with positive people and to encourage and compliment others. We fragile beings need nurturing and praise. Finding fault takes no talent, no education, no special skills.

Every day, I exercise to keep this foot in shape. I know that a daily walk with a foot that has been fused in three places is not an option, but I do have to find a way to keep it from becoming stiff. My doctor and I decided the best exercise for my foot and for me is to swim twice a week. This also does wonders for my energy!

I've also decided to teach myself to play the violin. This task is ongoing, and I am determined to succeed. I also want to learn to play the mandolin and the banjo. I've mastered the panpipe, but so far the requests to perform have been scarce!

Today I also work part-time. The Minnesota School of Business established a campus in Moorhead in 2008, and I started teaching an evening class in the spring of 2009 in business and paralegal studies. What an incredible opportunity to be in the classroom with the most important people of all—the students. They deserve the best, and nothing less is acceptable. I aspire to be the very best teacher I can be every time I am privileged to be there.

Finally, I vowed to write a book documenting my experiences and the revelations of God working in my life that have forever changed my attitude, my conduct, and my very soul, and here it is.

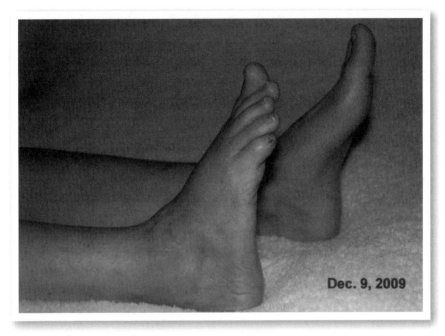

View of both feet, December 2009

Here I am walking in the backyard with my granddaughter, Jayah, July 3, 2010